THE
SECOND NINETEENTH

BEING THE HISTORY OF THE
2/19TH LONDON REGIMENT

BY
MAJOR F. W. EAMES

LONDON :
Waterlow & Sons Limited, London Wall
1930

THE
SECOND NINETEENTH

BEING THE HISTORY OF THE
2/19TH LONDON REGIMENT
DURING THE GREAT WAR

BY
MAJOR F. W. EAMES

The Naval & Military Press Ltd

Reproduced by kind permission of the Central Library,
Royal Military Academy, Sandhurst

Published by
The Naval & Military Press Ltd
Unit 10, Ridgewood Industrial Park,
Uckfield, East Sussex,
TN22 5QE England
Tel: +44 (0) 1825 749494
Fax: +44 (0) 1825 765701
www.naval-military-press.com

© The Naval & Military Press Ltd 2005

In reprinting in facsimile from the original, any imperfections are inevitably reproduced and the quality may fall short of modern type and cartographic standards.

To the Memory of his Comrades of 2/19th London Regiment who gave their lives for their Country in the Great War this book is dedicated by

THE AUTHOR.

INTRODUCTION.

THIS is a simple narrative of the doings of 2/19th London Regiment during the Great War, compiled by some of those who took part in them. As the years roll on it is inevitable that memories become blurred and it is hoped that this plain account will serve as a frame on which members of the Regiment may hang their more intimate and personal recollections; it may also be acceptable to some not directly concerned with the Regiment, who are interested in individual members or in the share of this London unit in the events of the years 1914 to 1918. It makes no pretence to literary distinction, nor does it seek to follow in the line of psychological studies of the British soldier on active service.

Just as, when it was in being, the secret of the Battalion's success lay in its "team-work" rather than in brilliant individual exploits, so have many willing hands contributed to the material embodied in this book. It is impossible to mention by name all those who have put at disposal diaries, letters, etc., but thanks are due to them one and all. The task of collecting and collating this material has been undertaken by Capt. C. F. Ashdown, and it is not too much to say that without his unbounded enthusiasm and untiring effort the book would never have been. Very valuable too has been the share of Mr. R. H. W. Case whose unobtrusive but none the less assiduous and effective work has been directed to making good the more glaring of the author's faults. In particular he is responsible for Chapters X, XI, XII and XIII. Mention must also be made of the unfailing encouragement and inspiration given, as in testing days fifteen years ago or more, by Capt. C. N. Radcliffe.

Thanks are due to O.C. 19th London Regiment for the loan of the block of the Regimental Colours which appears as a frontispiece and to O.C. London Scottish for permission to reproduce the inset map of Palestine. The map of 180 Brigade Sector, facing page 28, was reproduced from "The Second Twentieth" and the illustration facing page 39 is an Imperial War Museum photograph—Crown copyright. The "History of the 60th Division" written by Colonel P. H. Dalbiac, and "The Second Twentieth," the history of 2/20th London Regiment, written by Capt. W. R. Elliott, have proved of value as works of reference.

F. W. E.

September, 1931.

CONTENTS.

Chapter.		Page
I.	Formation and Training	1
II.	In the Line in France	19
III.	Crater Fighting	31
IV.	Salonika	42
V.	The Vardar Sector	49
VI.	Through Egypt to Palestine	59
VII.	Preparing for the Attack	68
VIII.	Beersheba and Sheria	76
IX.	Nebi Samwil	87
X.	The Capture of Jerusalem	93
XI.	Life in the City	104
XII.	The Defence of Jerusalem	114
XIII.	Talat ed Dumm	124
XIV.	The First Jordan Raid	132
XV.	Second Jordan Raid	142
XVI.	Reorganisation and Final Victory	148
XVII.	The Last of the 2/19th	156

APPENDICES.

Appendix	I.	Casualty Lists	165
,,	II.	Honours and Awards	183
,,	III.	Diary, 1914—1918	185
,,	IV.	Diary of a Prisoner of War	191

Index	201–207
Lists of Illustrations and Maps	208

CHAPTER I.

FORMATION AND TRAINING.

Camden Town, where, in the High Street, are the Headquarters of the 19th London Regiment, is the very centre of the Borough of St. Pancras, the regiment's recruiting area. The borough is quite a typical section of London: stretching from the Bloomsbury squares in the south to the heights of Hampstead and Highgate in the north, from King's Cross on one side to Regent's Park on the other, it includes several of the bigger railway stations and goods depôts, great stores in Tottenham Court and Hampstead Roads, and the densely populated districts of Somers, Camden and Kentish Towns. Such was the district from which the 19th, and its predecessor the 17th North Middlesex Rifle Volunteers, drew their men. The unit had always been a "working man's" as distinct from a "class" battalion, and it had a very good record. A characteristic feature was the way in which successive generations of the same families followed one another through its ranks.

What was eventually to be the First Battalion was embodied under the Haldane Scheme on the day War was declared, very speedily recruited up to full strength, and moved to its war station at Hatfield in Hertfordshire. Recruits continued to offer themselves, and, although in the meanwhile the first units of "Kitchener's Army" had come into existence, it was decided in the last days of August

1914 to duplicate all Territorial Units. And so was born the 2/19th London Regiment.

Within a fortnight the battalion was recruited up to full strength with men of the finest quality; they were fully representative of the manhood of the borough and were drawn from every grade of society. One whole company—under the old organization, about 120 strong—was drawn from the staff of the Railway Clearing House: the other companies were more heterogeneous in composition, but not a whit inferior in quality. Practically all the local trades and occupations were represented, not excluding the staff of the Zoological Gardens. Comparatively few had any previous experience of military life, and the great difficulty was to find suitable officers and N.C.O.'s. The question of command was very happily settled by the appointment of Lt.-Col. E. J. Christie. He had had about fifteen years' service, including the South African War, in the Royal Irish Rifles, followed by a term as Adjutant of the 17th North Middlesex R.V., the predecessors of the 19th, and on retirement from the Army he had taken over command of the battalion. Both as Adjutant and as Commanding Officer he had been conspicuously successful and immensely popular, and his double experience as professional soldier and in civil life made him ideally qualified for command in a civilian Army. The C.O. of a unit, especially of a newly-formed one, can make or mar it, and the fine record of the 2/19th can justly be said to have been based on the solid foundation laid by Col. Christie.

The first task which faced him was to find, or make, officers and N.C.O.'s. Very fortunately he was able to secure the services of just the man needed to fill the all-important post of regimental Sergt.-Major, for a small nucleus of N.C.O.'s detailed from the First Battalion included Sergt.-Instructor W. Manning, one of the permanent staff instructors appointed to the battalion from the Depôt of the Middlesex Regiment at Mill Hill. And to him, almost by right, fell the honour. Well indeed did he deserve it, and the battalion was very fortunate in being able to retain him in this capacity right through the War until after the Armistice. It is the veriest commonplace that the N.C.O.'s are the backbone of the Army, and that the battalion was no invertebrate body was due in no small measure to the persistent, quiet, tactful and humorous efforts of Sergt.-Major Manning. And so between them the C.O. and the R.S.M. set about shaping officers and N.C.O.'s out of the material at their disposal, while at the same time they were responsible for the training of 1,000 men, nearly all new recruits.

There were a few serving or reserve officers of the battalion, notably Capt. E. J. W. Hatherley, who became Adjutant, and Capt. J. G. Stokes, who took command of " A " (the Railway Clearing House) Company, a few more with previous experience in other units—including the second in command, Major A. B. Hubback, who subsequently commanded a Regular Brigade in France with great distinction—and others whose experience varied from that of sergeant in the Cambridge University O.T.C. to nothing at all. But Col. Christie was no mean judge of character, and besides the keenness which was common to all, most of them eventually developed some of the qualities necessary in a soldier. And of course there was the Quartermaster, Capt. MacEwen, whose experience may be gauged from the fact that when first he joined the Border Regiment his full dress headgear was a shako; and Durward Brown, the M.O., who instead of humouring patients with imaginary ailments as he had been doing for years, found it difficult to cope with men suffering from real disabilities who pretended to be sound in wind and limb.

In the earliest days the battalion paraded at H.Q. and marched to Regent's Park for elementary drill and physical training. There were no uniforms, no arms, no equipment; only plenty of men and boundless enthusiasm. It was a marvel of ingenuity to draw up 1,000 men in the limited space of a drill hall and to extricate them in military formation, but it was successfully accomplished. But the physical condition of many of the men, and of the officers too, fell far short of their zeal, and drill at the double produced many casualties.

The first attempts at route marching were round the outer circle in Regent's Park, and even this proved too much for some. Col. Christie had always been a great believer in the efficacy of singing on the march, so much so that when he commanded the battalion originally they came to be known as "Christie's Minstrels," and it certainly helped to keep the battalion going in those early days. Before long, as the men became fitter, greatly daring, the climb to Hampstead was attempted and achieved, although one of the Company Commanders, a veteran of the South African War, completed the journey in a taxi-cab. On one occasion two companies, with Capt. Stokes in

Lt.-Col. E. J. CHRISTIE.

Lt.-Col. D. C. SWORD, D.S.O.

command, ventured as far afield as Totteridge, and halted for the midday meal in close proximity to the Orange Tree Inn. The rush of business so taxed the resources of this pleasant establishment that the junior officers were detailed to assist behind the bar, an event probably without precedent up to that time in the annals of the British Army.

The next stage was entered upon towards the end of October, when the battalion with several others was quartered in the White City. Here, amid incongruous surroundings, some attempt at military routine and discipline was made. The men were quartered in the cheerless precincts of the Machinery Hall; the officers, not very appropriately, occupied the Gallery of Fine Arts; the messing arrangements were in the hands of a well-known firm of caterers. Uniforms were gradually issued, though difficulty was found with some " outsizes." Only a few D.P. rifles were available, but training in field work, as well as close order drill, was carried out in such widely separated areas as Wormwood Scrubs, Hampstead Heath, Hyde Park, Wimbledon Common and Richmond Park, to reach most of which involved considerable marching. By this time the regimental band had been attached to the battalion, and with their enlivening strains many a long mile was covered. It was rather an amusing travesty of the soldier's life to begin with, but little by little the battalion found itself. Ordinary barrack routine was followed as far as circumstances allowed, and a rather nervous subaltern doing his first duty as orderly officer is said to have asked the Sergt.-Major at what time he had to inspect the " lying-in " picket. Several of the officers were found to possess considerable gifts as lecturers, notably E. W. Sheppard, a deep student of military history and strategy who has since the war written an excellent short history of the British Army. There was one officer, a native of a French-speaking British Colony, whose knowledge of the idiom of the English language was not very profound, but he was well up in Field Service Regulations and full of enthusiasm. On one occasion he was lecturing the N.C.O.'s of his Company on the attack as it was practised in those days, the salient feature being the building up of a strong firing line by successive reinforcements. As he went on he got more and more enthusiastic, and his English became more and more broken, and he wound up by declaiming with dramatic gesture " Now, remember, ze most important zing, ze most important zing of all, ze firing line must be properly fed up." One foggy December morning the battalion was training in Kensington Gardens, and when the time came to form up and return to the White City, the Colonel, having lost his bearings in the mist, marched the troops off in diametrically the opposite direction into Kensington Gore instead of into Notting Hill Gate, and had gone some distance before he realised that something was wrong.

When the battalion got back all was excitement. There were fears of a raid on the East Coast, and without delay all the units in the White City were rushed off by train to draw arms at the Tower of London. And what arms ! Not bows and arrows or halberds certainly, but diminutive and obsolete Martini carbines, which had been discarded by the Cavalry during the South African War. But another stage had been reached ; the battalion was armed! Not for long, however; the scare subsided after a few days, and the lethal weapons were withdrawn. It was one thing to issue arms to every man, but an inexperienced "Q" department found it quite another to collect them all in again. Some men had taken them home to amuse the children! One distracted colour-sergeant had to call to his aid a man who admitted to being a burglar in civil life.

By this time had set in a process with which the battalion soon became all too familiar. The First Battalion was being prepared for service abroad with all possible speed, and was weeding out unfit men, under-age boys, and men enlisted under the original Territorial engagement for home service only. These were transferred to the Second Battalion in exchange for drafts of the best officers and men available, with results, as may be imagined, not at all advantageous, for the time being, to the average quality and morale of our unit. But it was the fortune of war. Thanks largely to the wise policy of Col. Christie, who insisted on keeping a nucleus of the original officers and men, the new elements were gradually absorbed, and the battalion succeeded in preserving its individuality.

As Christmas approached, there was some renewal of the invasion scare, and the leave regulations became much more strict; in fact, on Christmas Day leave was stopped entirely, and a rather dreary day would have dragged itself out devoid of any sort of interest had not the "fire alarm" been sounded just before midnight. Very few had ever heard the call before, and not all of them recognised it, but, of course, everyone had to turn out in various stages of deshabille, and hang about until the "all clear" was given. Whether there was really a fire or not nobody ever knew.

In the course of its training in the areas mentioned the battalion was frequently inspected by distinguished generals, and it must be confessed that neither officers nor men had at that time developed the proper sense of awe due to a "red hat." On one occasion in Richmond Park the redoubtable Sir Francis Lloyd, while watching the troops at work, sent for the officer in charge of one of the companies. This happened to be one who, although he subsequently proved himself a fine soldier and commanded the battalion in action, was at that time completely unfamiliar with the customs of the service. He ambled up, certainly saluted in a fashion, told the General he was glad to meet him, and offered to shake hands. "Frankie" Lloyd was not often at a loss for words, but the situation was too much even for him.

With the New Year a move was made to Reigate, where the battalion went into billets in private houses. This was a welcome change and, moreover, the surrounding country provided good opportunities for field training. It was at this time that the Signal Section came into effective existence, establishing itself as one of the most valuable elements in the battalion. At this stage, too, the four-company organisation was adopted. The new drill presented considerable difficulties and not least to those who were most familiar with the old. The four company commanders at the outset were Major O. F. Christie (brother of the C.O.), Capt. S. H. Bantick, Capt. Newman and Capt. Stokes. It should be added that by this time Major Hubback had been transferred to the First Battalion, which he subsequently left to command the 1/20th, and his place as second in command of the 2/19th had been taken by Major W. G. Carlton Hall.

Within a few days of the removal to Reigate the battalion, in common with scores of others in the neighbourhood, had to parade long before it was light one morning, and march to Epsom Downs. Here an immense concentration of troops was effected, for the purpose of enabling Lord Kitchener to show some distinguished Frenchman—said to be M. Millerand—that we really had got some troops in training. Quite early in the morning snow began to fall, and it went on falling steadily all day, adding not a little to the fatigues and anxieties of the troops. The battalion was ordered to form up in " Mass," a manœuvre which it had never before attempted, and the footmarks in the snow betrayed only too clearly that some of the company and platoon leaders had been somewhat uncertain of their destination. But the continued fall of the snow had at least this advantage, that the devious courses of these wanderers were blotted out long before the great ones appeared on the scene.

If the climb up Reigate Hill in the cold grey dawn had been a chilly business, it was as nothing compared with the descent in the afternoon. By this time nearly a foot of snow had fallen; men were slipping and sliding all the way, and sometimes almost a whole platoon could have been seen on the ground at the same time.

An early but excellent example of the celebrated Army principle of " eyewash " was produced on the occasion of this parade. Each of the parading battalions possessed only a hundred rifles, issued just before the event, and it was therefore arranged that these should be carried by the front-rank men of the leading platoon of each company, so that as the distinguished visitor drove past in a closed car at thirty miles an hour he would be led to suppose that instead of a meagre 12½ per cent. the whole mighty host was fully armed.

The issue of rifles, which were of the Japanese pattern, was completed not long after, and some of the companies fired a musketry course at Hythe. They reported the weapon to be very accurate though unwieldy.

At this time the spy-mania was very prevalent, and the battalion was required to find parties to picket the roads leading from London to the coast. But their only catch was Mr. Horatio Bottomley, out on one of his recruiting expeditions. Trench digging formed a more laborious part of the training, and so seriously did some heathen sappers take their duties that it required all the diplomacy of the battalion's cricketers to dissuade them from siting a line of trenches across the beautiful pitch in Gatton Park. Over the trench system a guard was detailed at night, so that the troops might become accustomed to all the strange sounds one hears and sights one sees—or thinks one sees—on the countryside in the dark. So the manufacturing of soldiers went on ; but with it went a draft-finding process so rigorous that in less than six months from the formation of the battalion there remained, probably, less than 20 per cent. of its original men.

During this period the troops were billeted on the inhabitants of Reigate in private houses, and right well were they entertained. The foundation was laid of many lasting friendships between the townspeople and their guests, and few indeed were the cases in which any sort of trouble arose. There was one occasion when the good lady of the house hinted discreetly than she would like one of her guests transferred ; the company officer investigated the matter but could not find any sufficient reason ; he cross-questioned the Company Sergeant-Major, who, after some hesitation, blurted out : " Well, sir, fact of the matter is, the man's *venomous*."

About the middle of March, the First Battalion proceeded to France and the second line moved into their quarters at St. Albans. The billets were for the most part in schools or empty houses, rather a sorry contrast with the kindly hospitality of Reigate, but a stage nearer the front line. The opportunities for training were no improvement on those afforded by the North Downs except that there was a range available near by at Gorhambury, on the Earl of Verulam's estate. The departure of the First Battalion on active service intensified the demand for drafts from the Second, and this demand continued until, in the following autumn, the newly-formed third line became able to supply the men required.

In mid-May another move was made, this time by route march to Coggeshall in Essex. The distance of about fifty miles was covered in three consecutive days. The majority of the men had never before covered anything like this distance in full marching order, and, moreover, they were men who, for various reasons, had not been selected for drafts to the First Battalion. It is hardly surprising therefore that the march proved something of a nightmare to all concerned, and was probably one of the least satisfactory episodes in the battalion's history. The conditions at Coggeshall were a pleasant change in that the troops were billeted in hospitable private houses set in delightfully rural surroundings, but the opportunities for training were rather limited. Not only did the drafting process continue, but a further disaster befell the battalion in the transfer of a hundred or so men, including many experienced non-commissioned officers who had enlisted under the original Territorial Force engagement. To replace these comparatively experienced old soldiers, the first draft from the third line was received. They were immediately dubbed "War Babies," but youth was their only failing, and it is one that people soon outgrow. As a matter of fact, these mere boys for the most part developed into the seasoned warriors who carried the battalion through its varied and trying experiences of the next three years.

In the middle of July the battalion went under canvas with the rest of the Brigade in Hatfield Broad Oak Park, near Bishop's Stortford. This was the first time that the whole brigade came together in close proximity, and it marked another stage in the process of organisation for active service. The advent of so many raw and immature boys of course threw back the training to the most elementary stage, and the ensuing difficulties were increased by the fact that the drafting process had been applied very extensively to officers and N.C.O.'s as well as to the rank and file. The task of organising the training and at the same time welding the battalion into a corporate entity was therefore no

OFFICERS 2/19TH LONDON, SUTTON VENEY, 1916.

Back Row (L. to R.)—2/Lts. Giles, Toole, Lt. Carey.

Second Row—2/Lts. Williams, Radcliffe, Heaton, M. W. H. Roberts, Patrick, Lt. Porteous (M.O.), 2/Lt. Ashdown, Lts. Gambell, Elgood, 2/Lts. Bennett, Buttenshaw, Major Grey, Lts. Bendall, C. H. Harden.

Seated—Lt. & Q.M. Bleeze, Capts. Ward, Tennant, Capt. & Adjt. Hobson, Lt./Col. Sword, Major Torrens, Capt. Jenkins (Padre), Capts. F. W. Eames, Williamson.

Front—2/Lts. Andreas, Tabberner, Lt. J. Cross, 2/Lt. Playford, Lt. Schonfield, 2/Lt. Vaile.

light one, and it is a high tribute to Colonel Christie's capacity as a Commanding Officer that through all these vicissitudes his battalion never lost its individuality nor its belief in itself. In October, towards the end of the Hatfield Broad Oak period, the whole division was twice concentrated and undertook operations lasting over three days, under conditions approximating to those of active service.

Early in November the battalion moved again into billets in Saffron Walden, and for a couple of months enjoyed the ungrudging hospitality of its hosts. By this time great changes had taken place in the *personnel* of the officers. Capt. J. J. B. Cross had succeeded Capt. Hatherley as Adjutant, and the four Company Commanders were Major O. F. Christie and Captains Pommerol, Williamson and Eames ; and among the newly-gazetted subalterns were C. F. Ashdown, P. M. Bendall, W. A. Carey, C. N. Radcliffe and T. K. Tabberner, all of whom were to play prominent parts in the more stirring events in the subsequent history of the battalion. Nor must Sergt. Drummer Ratcliffe be forgotten, whose first claim to the battalion's gratitude was the evolution, out of rather unpromising material, of a capital drum and fife band. The signal section had all this time been coming to maturity, thanks to the efforts of its first commander, Lieut. V. A. Elgood (one of the original officers), and its one and only sergeant, W. Langlois. Saffron Walden is a stronghold of Quakerdom, but there was nothing of the austerity usually associated with that sect in the town's hospitality to the troops, which covered the second Christmastide in the battalion's existence.

The general situation by the end of 1915 was rather depressing. The much-vaunted Loos offensive had miscarried, and a state of stalemate had been reached on the Western Front; the Dardanelles Expedition had proved a disastrous fiasco; Serbia had been overwhelmed and Bulgaria had come into the War against us; in no quarter was there any immediate prospect of a definite decision being reached. The affairs of the 2/19th were little more satisfactory. In addition to the difficulties arising from the constant drain of *personnel* and shortage of *materiel*, there was a feeling of uncertainty abroad as to the destiny of the battalion. Would it ever become an active service unit, or was it doomed to be no more than a training depôt? Nevertheless, the battalion's spirit was not quite crushed out; and it was with a feeling of relief that all ranks learnt, about the end of the year, that the 2/2nd London Division, of which the battalion formed part, was to become the 60th, under the command of so celebrated a fighting soldier as General E. S. Bulfin, and to go to Salisbury Plain for a period of intensive training.

Thither, after a very short stay at Hertford, the 2/19th proceeded with the rest of the division about the end of January 1916. The training centre allotted was Sutton Veney, near Warminster, on the north-western outskirts of the Plain. The battalion travelled by night and detrained at Warminster at dawn on a Sunday morning in a snowstorm. The first glimpse of its hutments after travelling all through a bitterly cold night was not, in these circumstances, a very cheerful experience. All ranks were soon to learn the meaning of the term "intensive training." As already mentioned, a change occurred in the command of the division; the brigadiers' turn came next. Colonel H. W. Studd, of the Coldstream Guards, who had seen service on the staff in France and been severely wounded, assumed command of 180th Brigade, of which 2/19th formed part. The new brigadier belonged to a family which has provided England with a test match cricketer, the City of London with a Lord Mayor, and the Church with a devoted and distinguished worker in the mission field.

And the process of replacement did not stop there, for it was decided to appoint comparatively young regular officers with experience of active service conditions to command battalions, in place of the men—mostly middle-aged and without the same experience—who had hitherto commanded and, in many cases, raised them. This was probably inevitable, but it came as a great blow to the battalion to lose its Commanding Officer, and it was very hard on Colonel Christie, whose qualifications and experience were far superior to those of many of his fellow-officers, to have to hand over to another the work which he had carried through so devotedly in most disheartening circumstances. The new C.O. was Lt.-Col. D. C. Sword, an officer with about fifteen years' service in the Scottish Rifles, beginning with the South African War and including considerable experience on the Western Front. His orders doubtless were to " ginger up " the battalion; and with characteristic energy and thoroughness he proceeded to do so. It could hardly be expected that in these circumstances the new Colonel would leap into popularity. In fact it was far otherwise, and it was not until the battalion got into the line in France that it began to appreciate his splendid qualities as a soldier and a man.

Other senior officers to suffer the fate of Colonel Christie were Major Carlton Hall, Major Christie (brother of the C.O.), Captain Cross and Captain Pommerol, from all of whom the battalion parted with real regret. Their places were taken by Major Torrens, a regular officer of the East Surrey Regt., Major Gray, a Scottish Territorial, and Capt. Neville Hobson, who had served with the new C.O. and became Adjutant. Meanwhile the command of " A " Company had passed to Capt. N. R. D. Tennant who had recently been posted to the battalion from the Royal Naval Division, and that of " B " to Capt. F. Ward, an experienced Territorial soldier who had seen commissioned service with 1/19th in France. At a later date Capt. MacEwen was replaced as quartermaster by Capt. E. Bleeze, and Capt. Porteous, a New Zealander, became Medical Officer.

Mention must also be made of a very junior officer who left the battalion about this time. He was R. C. Roseveare, attached from the Somerset Light Infantry, and during the few months he was with us he won all hearts. A mere boy in years, and of a most charming personality, he crawled into camp one pouring wet night at Hatfield Broad Oak, absolutely worn out by his journey from the West Country, and spent the night in the guard tent; needless to say he had been directed by the authorities to the wrong Hatfield. It is some indication of the regard in which he was held by all ranks that at Christmas time at Saffron Walden his platoon, in defiance of King's Regulations, presented him with a very handsome hunting-crop, which unfortunately he had little opportunity of using. It was with real grief that the battalion learned when in France that its much-loved Rosie, after going through the inferno on the Somme, had been killed at Ypres.

For one reason or another other well-known figures were fated not to accompany the battalion on active service. C.S.M. Woollaston, after more than 30 years' service with the regiment, failed to pass the doctor—of course, he was years above the age limit—and to his intense disappointment was left behind. Another unfortunate was Sergt. Dollin who, as the result of an accident on the range, was totally incapacitated from further service.

The " gingering up " treatment continued without intermission, and it became doubtful whether it was really the best way to transform civilians into active service soldiers. Training began with physical jerks almost before dawn, and lectures, for officers at all events, went on far into the night. Even the piano was banished from the ante-room of the officers' mess. Leave of all kinds, even for the week-end, was almost unknown for all ranks ; and although on one occasion the C.O. told the assembled officers in the orderly room that he had persuaded the brigadier to increase the allowance of leave for officers, he added that it was only in order that he (the C.O.) might have the power to stop it.

There was little relief from the tedium of the training programme. An outbreak of fire in the officers' lines caused amusement except to the individuals whose quarters were involved. A much more serious outbreak in the R.A.M.C. lines adjoining those of the battalion was more exciting. A little time was squeezed out of the training programme for sport—football and boxing for the most part. The battalion turned out quite a strong football team, the full backs being two officers, shortly to prove their worth in more serious combats, who provided an ideal combination of ripe experience and youthful dash. But perhaps the episode which is most often recalled from this period was the exploit of one Pte. Rogers of " B " Company, who succeeded in translating a barrel of beer from the Sergeants' Mess to his own hut.

The battalion arrived on the Plain much below establishment, but was gradually brought up to strength. A strong draft arrived from the Middlesex Regiment; then most of the home service men who had been transferred in the previous summer came back, forming a very valuable nucleus of trained men; and finally a draft of some 250 men, volunteers from R.A.M.C. training depots, was posted to the battalion only a few weeks before its departure overseas. These men, who came from all over the country, were splendid material, but they were quite untrained in infantry work, and it was a tremendous task to push them all through a superintensive course of training, including musketry, in the midst of the final preparations for embarkation. But it was done; and so the battalion, after a chequered career of nearly two years, was brought to the point of being submitted to the supreme test of active service.

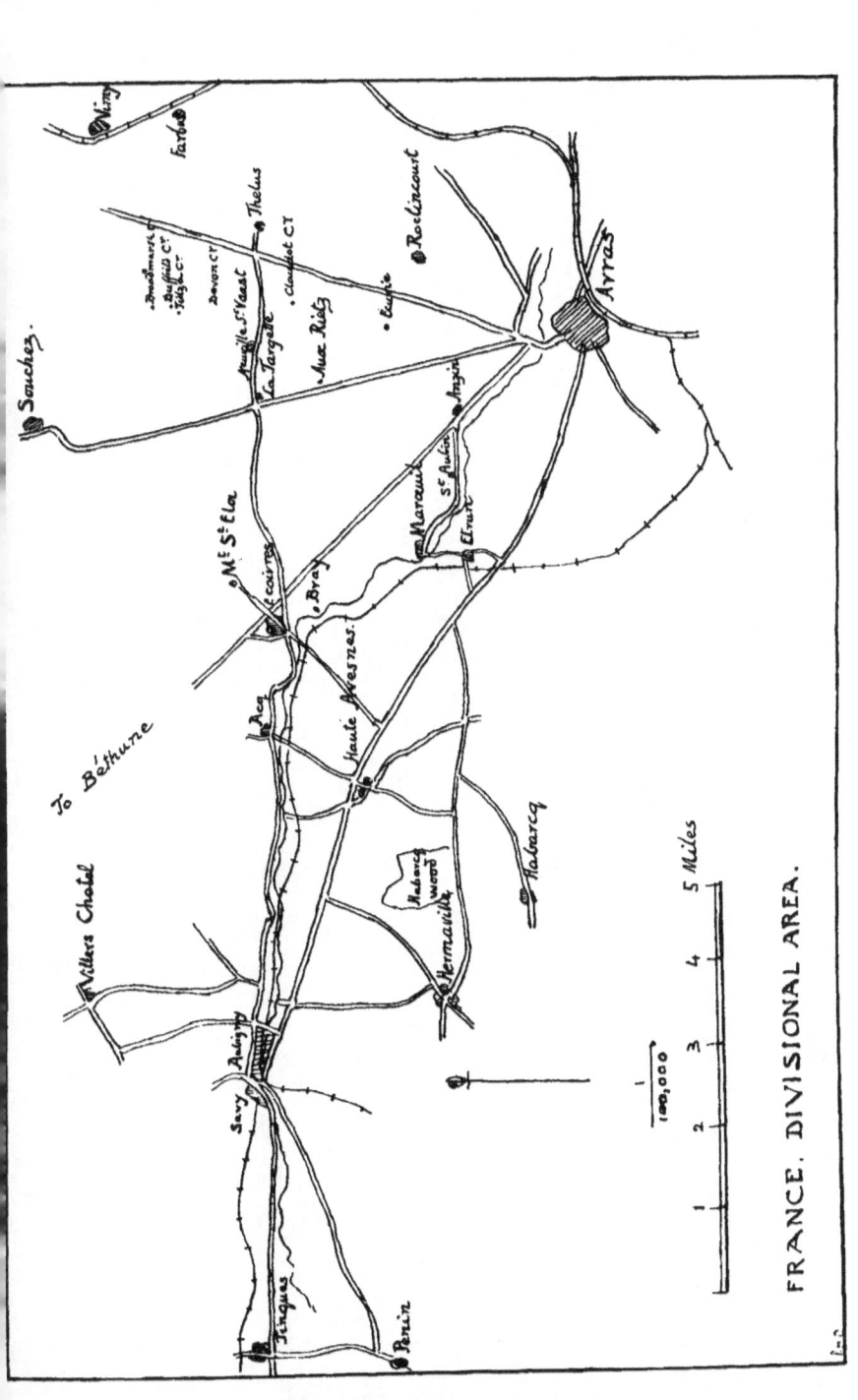

CHAPTER II.

IN THE LINE IN FRANCE.

And so on the morning of Friday, 23rd June 1916, the battalion marched out of camp at Sutton Veney *en route* for "Somewhere in France." For nearly two years it had struggled along, through good times and bad, moving from place to place in England; and thus everybody had become so accustomed to constant "moves" that this latest one seemed but part of the usual routine. But there were one or two unusual features. For one thing, with its numbers reaching 973 of all ranks, the battalion was practically at full strength, a state of things unheard of during the previous eighteen months; for another, clothing and equipment had been brought up to active service scale.

It was in no spirit of artificial enthusiasm that the men set out on this critical phase in the life of the battalion, nor was there any feeling of depression. It all seemed to come in the ordinary course of events, and everybody took it as such. It was rather sad to leave a few old friends behind, and they themselves were bitterly disappointed that they were not coming too.

The entrainment took place at Warminster and the first objective was Southampton. After the usual amount of waiting about at the docks the troops embarked during the evening in a small cross-channel steamer, and a smooth crossing was made during the night. By daybreak we were at the quay at Havre, and most of the battalion saw a foreign land for the first time. Naturally they found plenty to interest them on the quayside and during the march through the town to one of the rest camps on its outskirts. We at once got an impression of one of the seamy sides of war, for a party was forthwith told off to stand by to quell a threatened outbreak in a neighbouring detention compound. We lost no time, therefore, in realising that the dregs of an army always gravitate towards the base.

Very early on the following morning—it was Sunday—we marched down to the railway station and entrained. Another lesson was learned during the day, that a troop train in France never exceeds the speed of 10 miles an hour. All that day and most of the night we bumped and jolted along, past Rouen and Abbeville, and detrained towards dawn at Petit Houvin, a few miles south of St. Pol, whence we marched about four miles in a north-westerly direction to the village of La Croisette. Here the battalion occupied its first billets in France. Strict active service conditions were enforced, outposts being established by night at each end of the village with Lewis Guns covering the roads. Although the rumble of the guns could be heard, and their flashes and the Verey lights could be seen, the measures taken seemed excessive at a distance of nearly twenty-five miles from the front line. When, however, one remembers what happened later on, in March 1918, one feels that perhaps the precautions were not, after all, so unnecessary; at all events they helped to bring it home to us that we were getting nearer and nearer to "the line."

At this early stage in the active service career of

CAPT. N. R. D. TENNANT
"A" Company.

CAPT. F. WARD
"B" Company.

CAPT. C. S. WILLIAMSON
"C" Company.

CAPT. F. W. EAMES
"D" Company.

the battalion, Lieut. Ashdown began to take a prominent part in the battalion's activities. He had been detailed immediately on detraining to act as billeting officer for the battalion, an awkward job he had more than once performed very satisfactorily in England. In pursuance of these duties, he had to go with " M. le Maire " during the evening to one end of the village to arrange for the accommodation of a brigade of field Artillery ; and while thus engaged he was summoned immediately to the orderly room at the other end of the village. As was to be expected the message did not reach him very quickly, and in any case he had not acquired the art of being in two places at once, with the result that he found himself in the position of " while on active service, neglecting to obey an order," and his company commander was directed to put him under arrest. Fortunately the latter, and also Battalion H.Q., were rather busily occupied at the time, so the incident was allowed to sink into oblivion, and no firing party was ordered to parade at dawn.

Next day, Tuesday, 27th June, we marched off again to our next halting place, a village called Maizières. The distance was about eight or nine miles, but whether by reason of inexperience in reading French maps, or, as was officially suggested, because it was desired to accustom the troops to marching with full pack on the right-hand side of " *pavé* " roads, the distance we covered must have been nearly double. Lieut. Ashdown had again acted as billeting officer, with the assistance of three or four N.C.O.'s selected on account of their reputed knowledge of the French language ; in one case at least, however, knowledge was confined to that queer "lingua franca" which the British Tommy fondly believed to be French, and the French villagers had no doubt was English. Nevertheless, the billets were very comfortable and several pleasant days were spent here. The troops showed great interest in French village life, noticing in particular how calmly the people took it for granted that they should have a constant succession of foreign troops quartered upon them. Of the military situation little was allowed to transpire, and naturally enough seeing that the great Somme offensive was timed to begin on 1st July; but the growing volume of the artillery fire away to the south made us suspect that something was in the wind.

It gradually leaked out that the whole division was to take over from the 51st Highland Territorial Division, soon to make such a great reputation for itself on the Somme and elsewhere. The sector allotted was north of Arras on the south-western slopes of Vimy Ridge, the scene of terribly hard fighting by the French a year before. It became known that there had been great mining activity by both sides along the front and that crater fighting was a feature of the scheme of operations. Accordingly lectures and demonstrations on the subject were arranged by the XVII Corps authorities. Even in broad daylight, with everything carefully prepared beforehand and with no hostile artillery or machine-gun fire, it did not look much of a joy-ride, but we learned something of the technique of running out saps, establishing posts on the lip of the crater, wiring and so on. Other lectures and demonstrations were arranged for all ranks; the officers were addressed by the Corps Commander, Lieut.-Gen. Sir Charles Ferguson, who had been in France since August 1914, commanding first the 5th Division and latterly the XV Corps ; and also by Brigadier-General Charles, his Chief of Staff. A system of " rapid wiring " which required about thirty men to operate in close order, so to speak, was demonstrated by the Scottish Pioneer Battalion, and anti-gas, bombing, sniping, and other methods were dealt with.

Little by little we worked our way into the war zone. Two companies, " A," and " B," were moved up to work on repairs to communication trenches. Parties of officers and N.C.O.'s were sent on visits of inspection to the front line. This was, of course, the most interesting stage of all ; what was it really like to be in the front line trenches ? Everybody had heard so much about them ; would the reality correspond with the pictures conjured up in the imagination ?

The trenches were sited in a rather light friable soil, very apt to collapse. They were not very deep or well formed, and were dirty and rat infested. The Highlanders had not been there long, having taken over from the French only a month or two before. In the front line system there were generally two or three lines of trenches, with saps every hundred yards or so in front. No-man's-land varied from about 30 to 100 yards in width on the sector allotted to the battalion, and was dotted with mine craters along the front ; notwithstanding the convincing demonstration at the Corps School of how essential and easy it was to gain possession of both lips of a crater, it appeared that in practice they were held, one lip by us and one lip by the enemy. There were seven of these craters on the battalion front of about 1,100 yards. As the accompanying map shows, the front line trenches ran approximately north and south.

We had to take over from 1/5 Seaforth Highlanders, the northernmost unit of the Territorial Force. They treated us very well indeed. Every detail of the line and routine was explained to their opposite numbers and many useful hints were gathered, not all bearing out in their entirety the instructions given in the back areas. Perhaps the most valuable lessons we learnt from these fine Scots were conveyed not verbally, nor even consciously, but were gathered from their general demeanour, a blend of cautious vigilance and quiet confidence. Of course these hardened veterans—many had been more than a year in France—could not resist the temptation to pull the legs of the tenderfoot Cockneys; they waxed particularly merry at the tin plates which our fellows brought up with them, but all the same they did everything they could to put us up to the moves of the game so far as they knew them.

It was the middle of July when the battalion completely took over the line. The general scheme of the division was that each of the three brigades held about a mile and a quarter of line with two battalions in front line, one in support, and one in divisional reserve: the 181st Brigade was on the right, 179th in the centre, and ours, the 180th, on the left. After a few preliminary moves, reliefs were arranged so that each battalion spent six days in front line, six in support, six in front again, and then six in reserve. 2/17th Battalion relieved 2/19th and *vice versa* on the right of the sub-sector, roughly from Lichfield Street to Devon communication trenches; and similarly 2/18th and 2/20th alternated on the left from Devon Trench to Broadmarsh Crater. Battalions had all four companies in the line, in our case in order " A " " B " " C " " D " from right to left. The support positions were in the ruins of the village of Neuville St. Vaast and its suburb La Portique, and the reserve billets in hutments in the Bois des Alleux, under the shadow of the ruined twin towers of Mont St. Eloi. This notable landmark, the ruined condition of which was a reminder of the War of 1870, was about three and a half miles behind the front line. Rear Headquarters, that is the quartermaster's billets, were in the village of Ecoivres quite close to the reserve camp. From here, with battalion transport, the Q.M. picked up rations, stores, post, etc. from the Divisional Dumps at Haute-Avesnes and Hermaville. The Quartermaster Sergeants of the Companies took their respective shares at night, either by light railway to Chassery Dump near La Targette or by battalion transport to the cookhouse in Neuville St. Vaast. At either point they were met by the ration parties from the companies. The actual work of carrying rations, stores, ammunition, etc., through the communication trenches was terribly hard, for the trenches were narrow and twisting, and the surface was very uneven and covered with broken duckboards. One thing that surprised most of us was the extent to which the front line was depleted at night by the necessity of providing the numerous fatigue and carrying parties. It was usually only at stand to—daybreak and sundown—that anything like the full strength of the company was available in the line.

It was soon apparent that there was a lot of work to be done on the trenches to make them defensible and habitable. The wire in front was very sketchy, and at the earliest opportunity company commanders made arrangements for its strengthening. One of them took out a party of about twenty, as demonstrated at the Corps School, and proceeded according to plan; but—an occurrence that had not been provided for in the demonstration—an enemy sniper opened fire at about twenty-five yards range, killing a man at the first shot. It was decided to withdraw the party into the trench and consider a fresh plan; and thereafter it was found that a couple of good men working together, with the occasional supervision of an officer, produced much more satisfactory results. No-man's-land had to be explored by patrols, but it was very difficult to get a clear idea of the ground, broken as it was by numerous craters. Steady hard work had to be put in at the trenches themselves, deepening, revetting, and draining. Dug-outs were few in number and not very satisfactory, but work on them was beyond the ordinary infantry man without direction from the sappers and pioneers. Under their supervision great improvements were effected and several deep and comparatively spacious retreats were excavated. One of the most frightful experiences of company officers was the attempt to satisfy the insatiable appetite of the higher command for returns of every imaginable kind at all hours of the day and night.

All ranks settled down to the routine of trench life with surprising promptitude. Enemy activity mainly took the form of trench mortar bombardment. "B" and "C" Company fronts were particularly liable to receive this undesirable form of attention and they sustained many casualties from it. The official name for these projectiles was "Minnenwerfer," but the troops knew them by such appropriate nicknames as peardrops, rum jars, flying pigs, and generically as "Minnies." Our own weapons of this type, "toffee apples" manned by the Artillery, and Stokes Guns with Infantry *personnel*, were very effective. But the main hardship suffered by the men was sheer physical fatigue. Six days in the front line were bad enough, what with trench digging, ration parties, and innumerable other fatigue duties, not to mention wiring, patrols and the constant need for sentries to keep look out : the six days in support were even worse from the point of view of fatigue, for you were at everybody's beck and call ; and this was followed by another six days in the line. During all this time it was not possible to take off one's clothes or boots, so it may be imagined that after eighteen days of it the men were utterly worn out. The night of the relief, when we were to go back to the reserve camp in the wood, was one of indescribable joy, but for many the reaction was almost too much. Men often fell down from sheer weariness as they marched, and halts by the way were inadvisable lest the men should drop off to sleep.

The spell in reserve was made as restful as possible; baths and change of clothes were available—a tremendous boon this, and tribute must be paid to the efficiency of the organisation—recreation was provided by the Brigade Band, concert parties, informal sing-songs, whist drives, etc. Incidentally it may be recorded that at least one platoon of the battalion held a whist drive in the front line trenches. During one of the early spells in reserve the battalion was visited by representatives of the 1st Battalion, then lying a few miles to the north, and old friendships were renewed and much interesting and instructive information absorbed. All the preparations for the rest period were made by the Q.M. and his rear H.Q. staff, and their efforts contributed in no small measure to the high standard of morale the battalion maintained. The amenities of the neighbouring village of Ecoivres and of Acq and Aubigny a little farther back were also available and enjoyed by the troops.

There was one occasion when one of the men rather over-estimated his capacity to enjoy these amenities and was unable to return to camp. It was the night before we were due to go back to the line, and when he awoke he was apparently under the impression that the battalion had already gone up, and so set off as he was, without arms or equipment, to the sector which by that time he knew quite well. Of course he was reported as an absentee and as he was still missing when the battalion paraded, things looked black. It was the practice for company commanders and others to go up to the sector in advance, early in the afternoon, to take over and to have a look round in daylight. While the " deserter's " company commander was talking things over with his opposite number the latter asked why he had sent a man up in the morning without arms or equipment, for he could make nothing of the man's story. And so the incident closed happily—for a man who, even without orders,

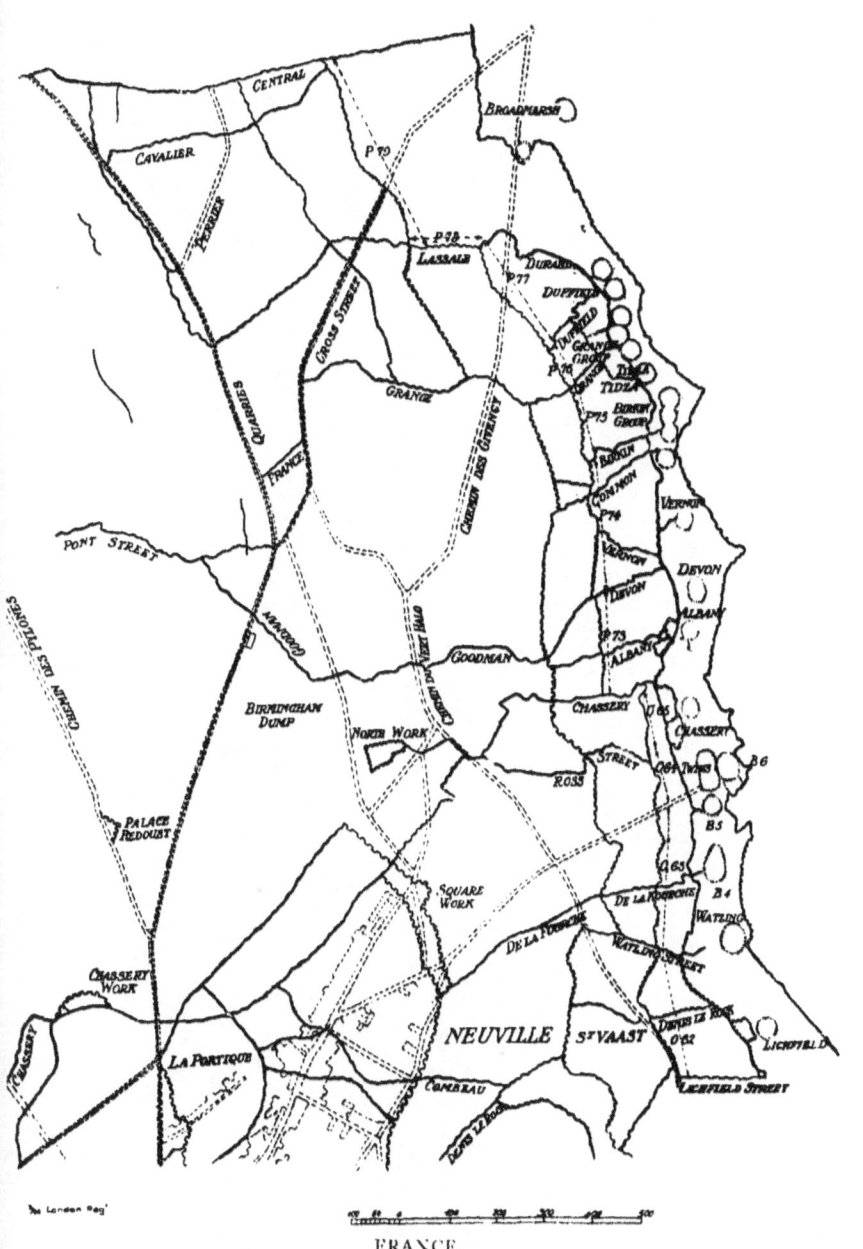

FRANCE.
180th BRIGADE SECTOR, VIMY RIDGE.

had acted as advance guard to the battalion, could hardly be charged with desertion.

The mining work was done by special Tunnelling Companies, one of which had headquarters known as the " Blue Pig " in the battalion sector. They were splendid fellows, marvellously efficient and with an astounding capacity for absorbing rum. They drew fatigue parties from a regular cavalry division in Corps reserve, and it seemed almost pathetic to see such famous regiments as 17th Lancers, Inniskilling Dragoons, and King's Dragoon Guards, engaged in the pedestrian task of humping bags of explosive and mine-spoil up and down communication trenches. Very close *liaison* was kept with the Artillery ; there was a F.O.O. (Forward Observing Officer) living in the line with each battalion, usually at one of the Company H.Q., and it was possible to get artillery support on any desired spot within a few seconds. Our own communications, back to Brigade H.Q. and forward to Company H.Q., were maintained by our own Signalling Section, and in spite of frequent damage by shell fire they were very seldom " dis."

The whole battalion organisation was controlled from Battalion H.Q. with extraordinary thoroughness. The C.O. was ubiquitous ; he knew every inch of the Battalion line, and wherever there was trouble, or some point to be settled, there he was sure to be found, ready with advice and encouragement. The Adjutant was just the same, and how he found time to get round as he did, in addition to his routine office work, was a marvel. The issue of ammunition and trench stores was the Sergeant-Major's department, and there, too, everything worked smoothly, although the first time he was in the line he was slightly wounded and had to go back for a day or so. And all the time rations, stores, post, etc. came up regularly every night: whatever else they suffered the troops were hardly ever short of food, usually much more varied and palatable food than could have been expected. The regular arrival of the post and parcels was a great boon and a triumph of organisation. Officers' Messes were able to get a certain amount of stuff, to supplement their rations, by private purchase, but not so much as might be supposed from some works of imagination recently published. For one thing the transport facilities were strictly limited.

Needless to say, superimposed upon the strenuous routine duties which have been sketched in this chapter, there were frequent hectic interludes more in accord with the popular idea of what War is like. Some of these will be dealt with in the next chapter. In the main, however, the lasting impression of life in front line trenches as we found it was one of monotonous, grinding labour.

"D" COMPANY H.Q. DUG-OUT, NEUVILLE ST. VAAST.

CHAPTER III.
CRATER FIGHTING.

The general situation when the battalion took over the Neuville St. Vaast sector on the slopes of Vimy Ridge in mid-July 1916 was that the Somme offensive was in full blast to the south of us, not more than fifteen miles away at the nearest point. A certain degree of success had been achieved, but not nearly as much as had been hoped for. A constant supply of fresh divisions had to be poured into the inferno with the result that other parts of the line were rather lightly held, and artillery ammunition was restricted by the insatiable demand for intensive bombardment and barrage in connection with the offensive. Similar conditions prevailed of course on the enemy side, for they had to concentrate considerable reserves in support of the hard-pressed divisions against which our attacks were launched and also vast reinforcements of artillery drawn from other parts of the line. Mine and counter-mine, trench-mortar and rifle grenade therefore were the weapons most in request on the Vimy Ridge. As has been said, there was a string of craters along the whole divisional front, and it was known that the enemy tunnellers as well as our own were still active.

In addition, therefore, to the work in improving the trenches and their defences, which was taken in hand as soon as we got into the line, stores were collected in anticipation of our having to undertake the consolidation of new craters should any be blown. It was not the intention of our own people to blow a crater on the battalion front, but enemy action was regarded as probable.

It was on the sector immediately to our left, held by 2/20th, that the first activity was shown by the enemy, and on 26th July, during the battalion's second spell in the front line, they blew a mine. Our people replied the following night with a counter-blast in practically the same spot. Much hard work and fighting resulted in our neighbours establishing themselves on the near lip.

About 10 p.m. on the evening of 28th July, just as it was getting dark, the enemy blew a mine on the extreme left of our own battalion's front near Devon communication trench. It came as a great surprise, for our own tunnelling people did not think that the works were in a sufficiently forward state. Lieuts. Ashdown and Tabberner of " D " Company, whose front it was that was concerned, were just relieving one another as officer of the watch when the whole earth seemed to rock and a good part of it go miles up in the air. It appeared at first that it was on the 20th's front again, to our left, but the two officers mentioned at once rushed up to the front from Company H.Q. by Albany communication trench, and met some wounded men coming down who told them that the left-hand post, No. 4, in charge of Corporal Morrison, had been blown in. Actually the mine was a few yards to the left of the post, otherwise all the men holding it would have been buried. Lieut. Ashdown took immediate charge on the spot and proceeded on the lines taught us a week or two before at the Corps School, so far as they were practicable. Lieut. Tabberner reported at Coy. H.Q. what had happened, and parties were at once organised to take up the necessary stores and to cover the working parties.

Almost immediately after the explosion the enemy artillery, trench mortars, and machine guns opened fire, and our own were not slow to reply. Our divisional artillery were amazingly prompt and accurate in responding to the request for "Rats," which was the code signal for retaliation. Of course the resources of "D" Company were completely used up, but support was speedily forthcoming from the other companies in manning the line against possible attack, and in providing carrying parties, both for the special emergency and for the normal necessary duties. Two sections of the battalion bombing-platoon under Lieut. Bennett were sent up from H.Q. to help in covering the working parties in the crater itself, who meanwhile were putting forth herculean efforts to establish our position.

The ground itself was naturally very soft after the upheaval. It was therefore easy to work, but terribly difficult to hold. Yeoman service was rendered by some of the tunnelling company in this department, perhaps as a gesture of apology for having misled us as to the likelihood of the mine being blown. Colonel Sword was early on the scene, encouraging and inspiring by his presence, but he found little occasion to alter the dispositions of the officers on the spot. He was accompanied by the Brigade Major, who was in a state of great excitement and showed a tendency to interfere with everybody. With some difficulty he was persuaded that it was his duty to proceed to the next Brigade H.Q. and report what had happened. All through the night the work went on at full pressure under a fairly continuous fire from weapons of all kinds, but happily the fire was not too well directed and casualties were not so heavy as might have been expected.

By dawn a deep trench had been completed from our front line to the lip of the crater, some 20 to 25 yards, and a post established in the lip itself. It was very important, though difficult, to secure some measure of protection for the post and trench by wire, and in gallantly attempting to do this in the early dawn by carrying out "knife-rest" obstacles, Pte. T. Hughes, a Welshman and one of the R.A.M.C. draft who joined the battalion a few weeks before embarkation, was killed by a sniper. With equal gallantry a mere boy named Whiting, who, it was subsequently discovered, was under age for active service, went out and brought in the body.

Much of the work had to be suspended at daybreak, but there was still a great deal that could be done in the trench in the way of revetting, deepening, etc., and there was little rest that day for the troops who had toiled so manfully throughout the night. With nightfall the efforts were redoubled and by the following morning the position could fairly be described as secure. The post on the lip of the crater had been strengthened and sandbagged and a sniper's plate installed; very fair wire defences were in position, mainly "knife-rests" and "gooseberries," names which very aptly indicate their character. The latter, which were more or less spherical in shape and about two feet in diameter, were very useful, for they could be made under cover in the trenches and thrown out in places where it was quite impossible to get out and do more formal work with pickets, or even to lift out "knife-rests." A considerable number of these "gooseberries" were thrown out into the crater itself and along the side to prevent enemy patrols working round. After this hectic period of thirty-six hours everybody concerned was naturally pretty well worn out, but all ranks could feel satisfied that the battalion had come through the first considerable operation in which it had been engaged with no little distinction. While all had done well, chief credit was due to the two " D " Company subalterns Ashdown and Tabberner, on whom from beginning to end had fallen the brunt of the immediate responsibility on the spot. The Brigade Commander, General Studd, visited the crater and works on the third day and expressed high approval of what had been done. It was typical of that fine soldier that in spite of the disability of lameness he should come to see things for himself; and equally typical that, after warmly congratulating the company commander on the achievement of his men, he should, on the way back to company headquarters, " choke him off " quite as wholeheartedly on spying an empty match-box in a " sump pit." Typical also of Army methods it was that immediately after he had been working with feverish energy for two whole nights and days, as described, Lieut. Ashdown should have been summoned to the orderly room to draw up a scheme of anti-gas defence, in which he had recently attended a short course of instruction.

The routine of trench life set in again after this episode, but the enemy trench mortars saw to it that there was sufficient variety. " B " and " C " Company fronts especially came in for attention;

a good many casualties were sustained, and much damage was done to trenches. The "Minnenwerfer" were the most formidable of these beastly contrivances; happily they could not traverse, so that unless by bad luck they happened to find a particularly vulnerable spot they did not do much damage. One day, however, they chanced to find "B" Coy.'s H.Q. dug-out and killed Lieut. Schonfield and wounded several others, including Capt. Ward, the company commander.

Ward was the life and soul of his company and beloved by the men; indefatigable in looking after their interests, he was nevertheless a very strict disciplinarian, and demanded and got a high standard of work out of them. Quite different in method was Capt. Williamson, his opposite number in command of "C" Company. His temper was inclined to be short, especially in the early morning, and he affected an air of complete indifference to the comfort and happiness of everybody but himself. Yet curiously enough his company was always as comfortable as it was possible to be in the circumstances. "C" Company understood their "Skipper" perfectly and took it quite as a matter of course that he should curse them uphill and down dale, knowing as they did all the time that he would never let them down and never ask them to do an unnecessary job, or one he would not do himself.

A fair type of "C" Coy. may here be recalled in Pte. Kelly. About 18 or 19 years of age, and —in spite of his name—a genuine Cockney, Kelly had all the characteristics of his kind; of rather poor physique he made up in grit and spirit what he lacked in strength. Once he was observed plodding along the communication trench, when most people thought they had got more than enough to carry, with the additional burden of an unexploded enemy shell perched on top of his pack. He was quite regardless of the possibility of its being detonated by a bump against the side of the trench, and blowing him to pieces. It would have been a splendid " Souvenir." While on duty one night in a post at the junction of the support line with Chassery communication trench, Kelly was killed with his two comrades in a sudden burst of shelling. It was always known afterwards as Kelly's Post.

As the terrific struggle on the Somme continued it became more and more necessary for G.H.Q. to know the dispositions of the enemy forces; and, to get information on this point, raiding the enemy lines, in the hope of taking prisoners, became general in every sector. One or two efforts had been made in our own division but without much success. At length 2/19th were ordered to undertake a raid on a fairly large scale. A party 60 strong was very carefully selected from the various companies, and three officers, Lieuts. Ashdown (" D " Coy.), Radcliffe (" C " Coy.) and Williams (" A " Coy.), who had already proved their worth, were put in charge. Capt. Hobson, the Adjutant, drew up very elaborate orders, which, as one would expect, left no point unprovided for and were afterwards quoted as a model for similar efforts. It was decided to make the raid from Lichfield crater, on "A" Coy.'s sector, in three parties, each with an officer in charge—Lieut. Williams on the right, Lieut. Ashdown in the centre, and Lieut. Radcliffe on the left. No-man's-land was carefully patrolled by small parties of the raiders for several nights beforehand, and the artillery carried out wire cutting at other places as well as the selected spot, so as not to attract unnecessary attention.

The night chosen was that of 30th–31st August. The party was to go lightly armed, some with bombs to establish blocks laterally and in communication trenches so as to prevent reinforcements coming up, or anybody getting away; some to act as moppers up of dug-outs, etc.; some to lie up on the parapet of the trench to watch for possible counter-raids and to take charge of prisoners; and some to lay out white tapes as they went, to guide the parties back. Almost everything worked splendidly; the artillery, trench mortar, and machine-gun barrages were admirably synchronised, and the centre and left parties carried on exactly to plan. The right party ran into a number of the enemy unexpectedly in a sap; Lieut. Williams was wounded and the Germans got away, except two who were killed. The other two groups spent twenty minutes in the enemy trench as arranged, and the bombing parties with the help of the barrage succeeded in isolating the sector. Sergt. Barratt had been selected to go with the centre party because of his knowledge of the German language, and he succeeded in persuading several prisoners to emerge from dug-outs in preference to being bombed. Pte. Rogers, the hero of the Sergeant's Mess beer-barrel episode, was chosen as bodyguard to one of the officers and armed with a battle-axe; but the combined effect of excitement and rum was such as to make him almost as dangerous to friend as to foe, and he was accorded the

A CRATER POST, FRANCE.

Imperial War Museum Photograph—Copyright reserved.

honour of taking back one of the first prisoners. He led his man by the ear and quite forgot the password when challenged on getting back to our line. But shouting " Souvenir " as he approached he was recognised, and he bumped his precious charge down into " A " Coy.'s H.Q. dug-out at the C.O.'s feet. Pte. Roberts took a prisoner single handed before getting into the trench at all.

It had been arranged to recall the parties by rocket signal, but the whole sky was ablaze with Verey lights, so that it was impossible to see the signals; after the agreed time, however, the parties withdrew quite successfully. Eight prisoners in all were captured; they were of 184th Saxon Infantry Regt. One was a Red Cross man, armed with two revolvers. The operation was rightly regarded as a great success and elicited commendation from Brigade, Division and Corps Commanders. Lieuts. Ashdown and Radcliffe, to whose good organisation and resolute leadership most of the success was due, were awarded the Military Cross, and Sergt. Barrett and Pte. Roberts the Military Medal. Only one man was wounded in addition to Lieut. Williams, and it was all of a piece with the good organisation of the show that the whole party was checked back into the trenches within a few minutes of the scheduled time.

During September preliminary orders were received to prepare for an attack on the Vimy Ridge, as an extension of the offensive on the Somme. Additional forward gun positions and " jumping off " places in the front line trenches were prepared; but nothing came of it all, and it was not till the following spring that the ridge—

how low and easy to pass it looked to us as we surveyed it from various observation posts !—was taken by the Canadians. It may here be recorded that the best chance that infantry officers got of seeing their own front comprehensively was when, as happened occasionally, they went to the artillery batteries for a day or two, " for instruction " as it was called, but really to cultivate a spirit of co-operation with the gunners.

About the middle of October it became known that the division was to be taken out of the line and relieved by one of the Canadian Divisions.

It was assumed that it was our turn to go into the Somme Battle which was still dragging on. In the last week of the month the battalion was relieved in support by 49th Canadian Infantry and for a week or more marched back to the neighbourhood of Abbeville, carrying out training in all the latest methods of attack when opportunity offered. On one occasion the battalion was inspected on the roadside by Sir Douglas Haig, the Commander-in-Chief. Finally the battalion reached Ailly-le-haut-Clocher—surely the most terrible tongue-twister for the Cockney Tommy—and settled down to final intensive training for the Somme.

But it was not to be : to the surprise of all, orders were received that the division was to entrain for Marseilles *en route* for Salonika. Time was short ; very few officers and men were fortunate enough to get home leave, and all was bustle and stir to get the battalion equipped for this next phase in its career.

Five months was the extent of our sojourn in France, and of course in comparison with that of most battalions it was short and uneventful. Nevertheless our casualties amounted to 200 and we left some 40 of our comrades in the little cemetery near Mont St. Eloi.

The journey by train to Marseilles was a most interesting experience and a few days were spent in that great seaport before embarkation. Its cosmopolitan character was a good introduction to the East, which was to be the scene of our activities for the last two years of the War.

CHAPTER IV.

Salonika.

After spending five interesting days at Marseilles we embarked in the Anchor liner " Caledonia " on 25th November. For the great majority it was their first experience of seafaring in a ship of anything like this size—nearly 10,000 tons—and it took some time to get used to the routine. Besides 2/19th, part of 2/17th and 2/18th were on board, and a machine-gun company, as well as the new brigadier and his staff. Gen. Carleton took over from Gen. Studd at Ailly, but did not take command of the troops on board, that duty devolving upon Colonel Sword. The men were fairly comfortably quartered on troop decks and the arrangements generally were good. Elaborate plans were made to meet the possibility of the ship's being torpedoed *en route*, a contingency not altogether remote, although a naval escort, British or French, was constantly in attendance. Altogether the experience was very pleasant and interesting. General Carleton took the opportunity to address the officers of the brigade who were on board, but it cannot be said that he made a very favourable impression; he was obviously of the *genus* " dug-out " and seemed to date from the pre-South African War period. He prefaced his remarks by saying that he had been given to understand that in civilian life most of his audience were civilians. A new acquaintanceship made during the voyage, and one which was to ripen into something much more intimate, was with

Colonel Norton, who had recently assumed command of 2/18th; the first impression he conveyed was of a reserved, studious man, carefully scanning maps of the country in which we were destined to spend the next six months. So far as we could judge, our course lay along the western coast of Corsica and Sardinia, across to and along the African coast, and then northward to the Archipelago. It was curious to find, however, that, reckoning by the sun, we were sometimes steering a course nearly opposite in direction to that of our destination; this occurred when there was reason to believe that we had been sighted by an enemy submarine.

Eventually we reached Salonika Harbour and landed on 1st December. As we marched through the city we got our first impression of the East. The populace was mixed Greek and Turk, picturesque but dirty; the same might be said of the city; the condition of the streets was dreadful. The allied cause was represented by troops of the British, French, Italian, Russian and Serbian Armies, irregular Greek "Venezelists," and British, French and Italian sailors as well. We marched about five or six miles over appallingly bad roads to a not unpleasantly sited camp at Dudular; this name, ludicrous to British ears, seemed to strike the keynote of the operations in which we were to be engaged for the next few months. During the fortnight and more spent here the battalion had experience of the vagaries of the Balkan climate, and the fatuity of the arrangements of the higher command. During the daytime it was sometimes pleasantly warm, like a summer's day in England, and training of the most formal kind was carried out; one operation, conducted in full marching order, was the assault on a precipitous hill, about 1,000 feet high, on much the same lines as were adopted with such disastrous results at Majuba in the first Boer War. The signalling officer gained great kudos for the battalion by the regularity and completeness of the reports he transmitted to Brigade H.Q. as the advance proceeded, but rumour had it that they were all carefully prepared and written out the day before. Except in the middle of the day the weather was cold; frequently there came from the mountains in the north terrific blasts of piercing wind, against which it was wellnigh impossible to keep tents standing, and then as a change came torrents of rain which made the camp a morass. Orders were issued for tents to be smeared with mud as some measure of concealment against aerial attack, but of course the rain washed all the mud off again. Efforts were made to improve the drainage of the camp by digging trenches to carry off the water, but the Brigade forbade it, and ordered that instead stone paths should be made through the camp. There were no stones available and no means of procuring them, and if there had been they would only have sunk into the mud, making the going worse than ever and doing nothing to remedy the trouble.

The native population, Greek for the most part, was reported to be none too friendly, and strict orders were issued that men were not to wander away from camp or associate with the civil population. Nevertheless one man—he looked as though he might have had a gipsy strain in him—disappeared for a couple of days, and came back having taken part in some wedding festivities in a neighbouring village. The attitude of the Greek Government itself was not at all satisfactory at this period, and one of our brigades, 179th, was sent away down near Mount Olympus to watch the pass into Greece proper and prevent any unfriendly concentration or movement. During the intervals of fine weather splendid views opened out before us, from the isolated snowclad peak of Mt. Olympus in the south to the lofty range which seemed to fill up the whole country to the north. Asked what he thought of this unaccustomed prospect one of our Cockney lads ventured the opinion that it was like an advertisement for milk chocolate. Some of the company officers tried to interest the men in the historical associations of the countryside, with special reference to Alexander the Great, but to some the name only recalled the leader of a famous ragtime band.

A day or two before we were due to move up country, mules were issued to the battalion in lieu of wheeled transport. The animals were quite unbroken and the transport men unaccustomed to deal with them. Practice loading and treks were the order of the day, and at the first few attempts it was unusual for animal, driver and load all to return to camp together. But with that amazing adaptability which is so characteristic of the Londoner the difficulties were overcome, and before long the men and their new comrades were on thoroughly good terms. Meanwhile the furious barrage of the paper war went on with greater fury than ever; one day's bag of "nominal rolls" demanded of companies included (*a*) clerks and typists, (*b*) men with broken tooth-plates, (c) men with broken spectacles, (d) men not vaccinated since the outbreak of war. During all this time rations were short and lacking in variety, presumably as a result of enemy submarine activity. We heard with regret that the good ship "Caledonia," in which we had voyaged from Marseilles, had been bagged on the return trip, and the Captain and a General taken prisoner. There was, however, no loss of life.

On 18th December the march up country began. The first stage—only eight miles—took us to Naresh. It does not sound much but the road was unimaginably bad, and the men were carrying a crushing load. In addition to the ordinary marching order with ammunition and bombs, a blanket, waterproof cape, bivouac sheet and pole, and "the unconsumed portion of the day's rations" were all piled on somehow or other. Including clothing, arms and equipment, the load totalled all but 100 pounds; and remembering that many of the "men" were actually half-grown weedy lads, it will be realised that many of them were carrying more than their own weight. The infliction seemed all the more inexcusable as the line of march ran parallel to a broad gauge railway on which familiar-looking English locomotives were working. It was with great difficulty that the march was completed, and with one accord company commanders reported at orderly room that it would be impossible to go farther under such conditions. The Colonel was able to arrange for part of the load to be conveyed by rail on subsequent stages.

A pleasant site for the bivouac, with facilities for bathing in a stream, had been selected by Capt.

Tennant, who had ridden on in advance, but the march was resumed next day. A march of about the same distance, over roads worse if possible than those of the previous day, brought us to Salamanli, where another night was spent. The third march was slightly longer and the road certainly worse than ever; for considerable distances the men had to struggle through mud up to the knees. The bivouac was near Sarigol and everyone was thankful that the next day was to be a rest. Considerably refreshed by this relief the battalion marched on the day after their rest along the railway to Janes, where the bivouac was on the side of a hill close to an aerodrome. The march was continued next day to Mihalova Ford, where an ideal camping ground was found beside a pleasant stream. Luckily it was not till the following morning that we learned that the site was in full observation from a hill known as 535, which was in enemy hands and well within artillery range. Nobody had any idea that we were so near the front line. The following day was Christmas Eve, and a long march of ten miles, but over much better roads, brought us by about three o'clock in the afternoon to our immediate destination, Spancova Farm: this name, like Dudular, seemed to emphasize the farcical nature of the operations in this theatre of war.

Here, on a desolate windswept hillside overlooking Lake Ardzan, our first Christmas on active service was to be spent. There had been rumours of plum puddings sent out from home, but there were no signs of them, and no facilities for cooking them if they had been there. Difficulties of this kind, however, were easily surmounted. The cooks, in alliance with the Pioneers and with the active co-operation of most of the battalion, proceeded to construct ovens, more or less of the regulation Aldershot pattern. Lieut. Radcliffe, who had established a reputation as a raider in France and was now, not inappropriately, in charge of battalion canteen arrangements, set out, with wheeled transport put at our disposal by an A.S.C. Unit in the vicinity, to the big ration and store dump at Karasuli, five or six miles away. Late in the evening he returned with an amazingly varied bag, which included not only plum puddings, but turkeys, pork, a varied assortment of tinned stuff, and even a rum issue. As a result of this expedition, which in its way was quite as successful as the raid in France, the battalion spent Christmas in far more cheerful conditions than could possibly have been expected. The weather was fine and warm; a Church parade service was held with familiar Christmas hymns; the dinner was indeed a masterpiece in the circumstances, every man partaking of turkey, eked out with pork and plum pudding. In the evening a concert was held in one of the farm buildings. To this the Colonel and Major Gray, among others, contributed items, but the *pièce de résistance* was the issue of rum punch compounded by the Colonel. Later on the officers dined together as a mess for the first time since leaving England, and there was great hilarity and good fellowship, and, if anything, a little too much oratory.

CHAPTER V.

THE VARDAR SECTOR.

On Boxing Day we began to think about work again. The battalion was to be in Corps reserve to the 22nd (Welsh and Lancashire) New Army Division in the line. Lines of defences were to be dug, roads to be made up and drained, stone to be quarried, and a light railway to be laid. On 27th December "B" Coy., under Capt. Ward, went off on detachment to Vardino to start work on the defence scheme to the west of Lake Ardzan. A day or two later the senior officers went up to the front line, held by a battalion of the Welch Regt. which had previously been commanded by Col. Sword's brother. What a revelation the front line was ! We held the forward slope of a range of hills facing a corresponding range held by the Bulgars about a mile away, with a wide and rather deep valley between. The river Vardar was immediately to the west, flowing from the enemy direction towards us. The defences consisted of shallow trenches, not completely linked up, something like sangars, with plenty of wire in front. All the dugouts and bivouac areas were on the reverse slopes of the hills, and the trenches were only manned by night, with a few look-out men by day. It seemed quite the recognised thing for officers to wander about in the open on the forward slope in broad daylight, even in front of the wire ; and except for a stray pipsqueak or long-range machine-gun burst, the enemy took no notice. Transport came right up to Coy. H.Q. on the reverse slope, so that compared with conditions in France the troops had an easy and comfortable time.

The naturalists of the battalion found much to interest them in the countryside. Game was plentiful near the lake; not a few jackals prowled round the camps; as the season advanced the millions of frogs in the swampy lakeside made an amazing uproar; butterflies, some of them very rare in England, appeared as the weather grew warmer, and with the coming of spring the wild flowers added a touch of colour to the rather desolate scenery, which was mountainous and rocky. It was very interesting to see flocks of wild geese flying very fast and at a great height. In the early winter they went south, presumably from the Baltic and Polish marshes to Northern Africa, and in early spring they were seen returning. The flocks numbered forty or fifty birds in perfect V formation, led by an old gander who had probably been that way before.

There was practically no native population anywhere near the front line, but a few civilians of unprepossessing appearance hung about Karasuli and similar places. There was one lad who used to hawk the *Balkan News*, the excellent broadsheet issued by G.H.Q., who was very proud of his command of the English language. One day he came through the lines calling " Varry good news British Battleship sunk " : presumably the goodness of his news consisted in its accuracy. Capt. Tennant organised some very successful concerts, perhaps the most enjoyable items in which were mouth-organ competitions; the Londoners are great experts on this instrument. Eventually the whole battalion, except "D" Coy., moved over to Vardino to work on the defences. The detached company continued work on the road and light railway and in the quarry; the trucks of stone were run by their own weight down the ravine in which the stone was quarried, and if they rounded the sharp curve at the bottom went on a quarter of a mile or so along the level beside the lake. But as often as not they tipped over at the curve, and the progress of the work was much hindered. It was suggested to the R.E. Officer who occasionally came to see how things were progressing that it would be an improvement if the curve were banked up; to this he agreed and, after making elaborate calculations in his note book, gave directions for the work to be done with the inner rail uppermost. Fortunately there were men in the company who had worked on the railway at home and they soon got the job done in the right way with very satisfactory results.

A company on detachment enjoys certain advantages in freedom from interference by the higher command; it is a case of "out of sight out of mind." But there are drawbacks too. For instance, they lose the services of the regimental medical officer, and have to rely on those of the nearest medical unit. So unsatisfactory did this prove in the case of "D" Company that the company commander was authorised to act as M.O., and for some weeks he took his own sick parade and administered No. 9's and other more or less appropriate doses from the doctor's little black box. It can at least be claimed that nobody died under his ministrations, and after a little preliminary and not unnatural shyness at trusting themselves to the tender mercies of a layman the troops began to suspect that the practice of medicine was not such a complicated business as they had imagined.

All through January and February the weather became steadily worse. Every night a bitterly cold wind blew from the north so fiercely that it was a matter of great difficulty to keep the tents standing; the best way was to dig down about a couple of feet and pitch the tent in the excavation, but of course provision had then to be made for drainage. About this time news arrived that Col. Sword had been awarded the D.S.O. in recognition of services in France; the battalion was very pleased, realising that it was a recognition not merely of the C.O.'s fine soldierly qualities, but of the battalion's response to them as well. Such diversion as was possible was provided for the troops; canteen stores were fairly plentiful, considering the number of ships that were bagged by the enemy submarines.

The conditions in which the men lived made it very difficult to avoid trouble with lice, but the efforts were fairly successful; baths and cleansing equipment for clothing were available and much appreciated. Football matches were arranged and on one occasion Capt. Hobson, the Adjutant, who was nothing if not rigid in his adherence to forms and military routine, drew up regular " movement orders " for the battalion team when they went to play against another battalion some miles away. Some thought that he should have supplemented them with " operation orders " for the conduct of the game itself; but as he played centre forward himself, and scored the winning goal, the omission was overlooked.

Towards the end of February there was a scare that the enemy were going to attack on 1st March, and the brigade was concentrated near Caussica, at the north end of the lake, in reserve to 65th Brigade of 22nd Division. The move was made on the night of 28th February and it synchronised with the worst blizzard of the whole winter. A miserable night was spent, without blankets, and under orders to move at any moment. Our cooks and Q.M. surpassed themselves on this occasion by providing hot cocoa at frequent intervals, and the battalion suffered but little. In this they were more fortunate than two other units in the brigade, who had hundreds of cases of frostbite. The alarm came to nothing, but it transpired that we were shortly to take over a section of the line.

On 8th March, after a week spent mostly in training, the battalion made a short move to take over from 9th S. Lancs. in divisional reserve near Caussica Station. The weather continued bad with the same piercing winds, but rain instead of snow. Training, alternately with work on ammunition dumps, was the usual programme. Parties of officers went up to see the sector we were to take over on the left of Reselli, which was quite unfamiliar to us. The sector was cut across roughly north and south by two ravines called Selimli and Cidemli, separated by fairly steep hills which sloped down to the wide valley that constituted no-man's-land from the Vardar eastwards; it was hereabouts a couple of miles across to the enemy positions on the hills on the other side. About this time the enemy began to use gas shell, and there was great output of paper to ensure that every man put on his respirator on the slightest provocation.

On 18th March the battalion suffered what was afterwards known as its "pleasant Sunday afternoon." Three flights of enemy 'planes spotted a convoy on the main road that passed near our camp, and bombed it severely, not omitting to drop a few on us. Luckily we were able to get our men into the newly dug ammunition dugouts and slits, but the convoy suffered badly. Curiously enough it was commanded by our old friend Capt. Pommerol, who was immensely proud at having a button torn off his jacket by a shell splinter. Fine work for the wounded was done by Capt. Newton, our new M.O., and by Sergt. Langley, his medical orderly, who was awarded the D.C.M. for his services on this occasion. During the *strafe* about 50 men, with three officers of "D" Coy., were crowded into one of the ammunition recesses, and a bomb dropped about 30 yards from the edge of it. The concussion was terrific and the air was filled with smoke and dust; the first word was spoken by Lieut. Bencher, who had never been known to get excited or rattled; quite calmly he remarked to his fellow-subaltern "Curse you, Henderson! you've trodden on my corn."

On the night of 19th March the battalion took over the front line from a Lancashire battalion, under a fairly heavy bombardment of gas shell. "A" and "C" Companies were in front line, but the support companies had to find large parties at night for what were called fighting patrols; their function seemed to be to lie a hundred yards out in no-man's-land, obstructing the field of fire from our forward positions. There was no sign of enemy activity, except sporadic bursts of gas shell. It all seemed very unreal and it was difficult to take things seriously. One night Capt. Williamson, commanding " C " Coy., who had proved in France his coolness and resource in emergency, was warned from another unit that an enemy patrol, estimated at 150 strong, was moving along the front towards his position. He was by no means alarmed, and suggested to a brother company commander, who happened to be in his H.Q., that they should go and look for them. So out they went, Capt. Williamson without arms or equipment and wearing slippers, and satisfied themselves that what had been seen was the rows of pickets for wire which assumed fantastic shape in the moonlight.

About this time rumours began to gain currency that a considerable offensive movement was in prospect, and that our share was to take the form of a feint attack on the " Nose " and " Crête des Mitrailleuses," two commanding positions in the enemy line quite near the River Vardar. On the night of 27th March the battalion was relieved by 8th South Wales Borderers and moved away to the left to Oreovica near Smol village, behind the sector where it was planned that we should make our effort. The night was very dark and the tracks bad, so that some companies were very late getting into their new quarters and some of the transport came to grief. Preparations for what turned out to be little more than a raid went on actively. A practice course was taped out ; parties went up to the front and reconnoitred the ground ; men were practised in the handling of Bangalore torpedoes, which were long cylinders about 10 feet by 9 inches, full of H.E., which were to be exploded in the enemy wire. On 5th April the enemy carried out a big, and unhappily very destructive, air-raid on the dumps at Karasuli, causing serious damage and loss of ammunition. As a result our part in the proposed operations was cancelled, and on the night of the 7th the battalion moved back into reserve at the Crag near Spancova. Two companies, "A" and "D," were detached in support to the 2/17th and 2/18th respectively. "D" Coy. had a very comfortable camp in Lothian Ravine, through which flowed a little stream that provided good facilities for washing; it was even possible, by damming the stream, to make a practicable swimming bath, and this of course was a great boon.

The proposed offensive was postponed, on account probably of the shortage of ammunition caused by the Karasuli air raid, but towards the end of the month operations began. The 22nd and 26th Divisions attacked Hill 535, and 2/20th made their raid on the "Nose" with which our effort was to have been combined. This latter was intended only as a diversion to the main attack and may have been successful in this respect, but the casualties were heavy and the tangible results *nil*. Capt. Watson, who was in command, gained a very hard-earned M.C. On the night of 27th April the battalion, reunited, took over I Sector on Waggon Hill from 2/15th London. The move was made in pouring rain and over very difficult country, but was completed without serious mishap. The new position was a pleasant one; the front line companies,

"A" and "D," held the forward slope of Waggon Hill facing across a valley four or five miles wide to the enemy position on the next ridge, with their bivouac area on the reverse slope; the other two companies were in support in very pleasant ravines. A curious feature of the line was that the deserted village of Sejdelli lay about half a mile in front of our forward posts; it was not occupied by our troops, but was a happy hunting ground for foraging parties in search of wood, etc. With the advance of spring the countryside took on a delightful aspect. Wild flowers were in profuse variety, and bird life was equally interesting.

The major operations against Hill 535 were still dragging on, but it was generally known that they had not met with much success; the enemy positions were well nigh impregnable if held with determination, and our artillery support was inadequate. Our activities consisted mainly in improving our already strong positions and in sending out huge patrols to wander more or less aimlessly in the four or five mile stretch of no-man's-land. After several false alarms the battalion was relieved on 17th May by a battalion of Argyll and Sutherland Highlanders, and moved back to Mihalova for "training." This seemed to presage a further offensive, but rumours soon began to fly round that we were destined for another sea voyage. Orders and counter-orders followed in rapid succession, and after a preliminary move back towards the line near Lake Doiran we started on 1st June to march back, in the greatest secrecy but with the Brigade Band playing, towards Salonika. We reached Dudular again on 5th June, doing most of the marching by night ; the roads were now in good condition, in contrast to what we had experienced six months before. After further delays, during which we were very busy changing from Macedonian to Egyptian establishment in equipment, we eventually sailed from Salonika Harbour on the morning of 10th June. Our feeling as we departed was one of profound relief that we had got away from this pestilent theatre of war without encountering serious misfortunes or becoming involved in the slow process of demoralisation that seemed to overtake everybody who remained there for any considerable time.

CHAPTER VI.

THROUGH EGYPT TO PALESTINE.

Curiously mixed were the battalion's feelings as we steamed away southward from Salonika Harbour that sunny morning in the good ship "Minnetonka." She was a big boat, nearly 13,000 tons, but very crowded; nevertheless the change of routine came as a relief to the men, and the voyage, as an experience, was quite enjoyable. Everybody too was delighted to get away from Macedonia, where it was impossible to avoid the impression that it was a "dud show" and not easy to escape the consequent tendency towards gradual demoralisation. But what next? Was the battalion ever to achieve anything of note in this heroic epoch? During the few months spent in France we seemed to be feeling our feet, and took it for granted that in due course we should be subjected to a more fiery ordeal; but just when we thought we were destined for the supreme test on the Somme we were spirited away—not, be it admitted, without a profound feeling of relief—to Salonika. This act in the drama was frankly an anticlimax, and we could not help wondering whether the next was to be another side-show, whether we were really to merit the nickname, which the division had acquired, of "Bulfin's Circus."

It had come to be known that we were to join the Egyptian Expeditionary Force, at this time hung up in front of Gaza. Was this another stalemate in which we were to be involved? The first attack at Gaza in the spring had barely failed of success:

but the second, a few weeks later, had been a disastrous and humiliating failure. The *morale* of the troops was severely shaken, and we did not want to be mixed up in another futile and badly managed enterprise.

Such thoughts, although we did not admit it, were smouldering away somewhere at the back of our minds, but meanwhile we laid ourselves out to enjoy our brief sea trip. We threaded our way through the islands of the Archipelago, which presented a very rocky and picturesque appearance ; our escorting destroyers were very active and assiduous, for it was known that the " U " boats were busy and they were suspected to have secret haunts among the islands. Passing Crete, to the west, we sighted Alexandria on the afternoon of 12th June. From afar the view of the city, enveloped in the haze arising from the surrounding desert, looked distinctly oriental, but as we approached it became apparent that much of the building was quite European in style, and the docks into which we steamed were much as other docks, with quays and warehouses and railways complete.

We were to have no chance of inspecting the city at close quarters, for we went direct from ship to train, and by evening were *en route* for Moascar, near Ismailia, on the Suez Canal. We stopped once or twice during the night at wayside stations, and each time heard the monotonous cadence of the Arab speech, which was soon to become so familiar. The predominant cry sounded to our ears like " eggsakoo," and we soon realised that it was no native word, but the businesslike Arab's effort at " hard boiled eggs," in which articles he drove a thriving trade with our fellows. The first train reached its destination about three in the morning, and the troops were led a mile or so in pitch darkness to the camping area, which appeared when dawn broke to be nothing but an endless expanse of sandy desert, with a few skeleton permanent buildings here and there. But equipment and stores of all kinds were quickly available, and a frenzied day was spent in pitching a tent-camp in such heat as few of the men had ever experienced before. We soon found that there were amenities of various kinds in the immediate neighbourhood. Not only were there good canteens at the adjoining Australian Base Depôt and enjoyable bathing in the salt lake near by, but Ismailia, only two or three miles away, was a town with a European quarter which included a first class club, primarily intended for the officials, mostly French, of the Suez Canal. All ranks thoroughly enjoyed themselves, and a few lucky ones were granted leave for a day or two to Cairo. In their wildest dreams our Cockney lads can hardly have imagined that they would ever have the chance to see the Pyramids, the Sphinx, and the veritable mummies of the ancient Pharaohs in their native setting.

These pleasant incidents were but a symptom of the changed conditions in the whole E.E.F. Command had been taken over by Gen. Sir Edmund Allenby, under whom our Division had served for a time in France, and his first task was to restore and improve the *morale* of the troops. He gave vastly extended facilities for leave to Egypt, encouraged in every way sporting and amusement activities, and arranged for much greater supplies of canteen stores and supplies generally. In this way he soon had the troops feeling on much better terms with themselves and at the same time he was pressing for large reinforcements in 'planes and heavy guns and ammunition. As these were forthcoming it was soon evident that something was afoot, especially as another Division, the 10th (Irish), was known to be under orders to follow us from Salonika. Soon there was talk of Jerusalem by Christmas, but of course no one took that seriously.

Nevertheless there was an indefinable feeling abroad that there was real business to be done. The days at Moascar were mainly occupied in training and refitting with tropical kit, and of course some time was necessary for the troops to become accustomed to the climatic conditions. The heat was very great in the middle of the day, especially before noon, and even at night it was by no means cool. One frightful day was occupied in repitching the brigade camp so that the lines " covered off " from back to front, from side to side, and even diagonally; this operation was carried out in the full blaze of the midday sun, while the Brigadier supervised from aloft in an aeroplane. There were not many who did not add to their knowledge of the English language that day, and all acquired additional facility in its use.

It was part of the new order of things that recreation of various kinds should be encouraged. Bathing parties were organised and so were concerts and cinema shows, and even cricket matches on a very sandy pitch. There was one quite interesting game between teams representing the Brigade and the Australian Depôt, whose eleven included Cotter, the one-time test match fast bowler ; that the match ended in a draw was of course a proof of its approximation to first class standard.

On the evening of the 23rd June, being the anniversary of the battalion's embarkation at Southampton, the officers held a little dinner at the French Club in Ismailia, and with complete disregard of the King's Regulations, made a small presentation to the Colonel to mark the occasion. Nobody could help casting his mind back over those twelve months of varied experience, and perhaps the most interesting feature in the retrospect was the gradual—almost imperceptible—change in the feelings of the battalion towards Col. Sword. It would be idle to suggest that at the time we left England our sentiments were in the least cordial ; the most that could be said was that he had impressed us all by his zeal and energy. But as time went on, during the strenuous days and nights in the trenches at Neuville St. Vaast and in the rest camp at Mont St. Eloi, we came to appreciate the intense humanity of the man. What had seemed at first to be the incarnation of the military text books was found to be a creature of the same flesh and blood as our own, only so dressed up in the trappings of regular army tradition as to be almost entirely hidden from view. The Macedonian episode served to provide further opportunity to discover his loyalty, his humour, his almost childish exuberance of spirits as shown in his enjoyment of quite trivial incidents. And so it fell out that on the first anniversary of the birth of the battalion's active-service career it seemed quite the natural thing for the officers to commemorate the event in the way mentioned.

After a further period of training, refitting and acclimatisation the battalion marched off on the evening of the 5th July *en route* for the front. The line of march was parallel to the Suez Canal; it was of course in order to avoid the intense heat of the sun that the move was made by night. The first stage—about ten miles—was to El Ferdan, where a bivouac camp was pitched, consisting of shelters contrived from blankets, rifles, bayonets and string. The following evening we were off again, this time on a fifteen-mile stage to Kantara, the great base camp on the eastern bank of the Canal. In spite of the march being made by night, it was very trying, and the day's rest, again in blanket bivouacs, was very welcome. The camp was a vast wilderness with all the characteristics, some pleasant but mostly otherwise, of a base depôt. On the night of the 7th-8th the battalion entrained and travelled upwards of a hundred miles in trucks across the Desert of Sinai to Deir El Belah, not more than ten miles short of Gaza and at that time the railhead. The railway by which we travelled was perhaps the greatest achievement, up to that time, to the credit of the E.E.F. It had been laid immediately behind the most advanced troops, and on it they depended for practically every necessity of existence. Even water was brought up in great tank trucks until the completion of the pipe-line by which the waters of the Nile were pumped across the Suez Canal and the Desert, and afterwards, when the capacity of the pipe-line proved insufficient, the trucks were brought into use again. Another ingenious device that was adopted to mitigate the hardships of transport in the desert was the wire road, which consisted of layers of wire netting laid on the soft sand to

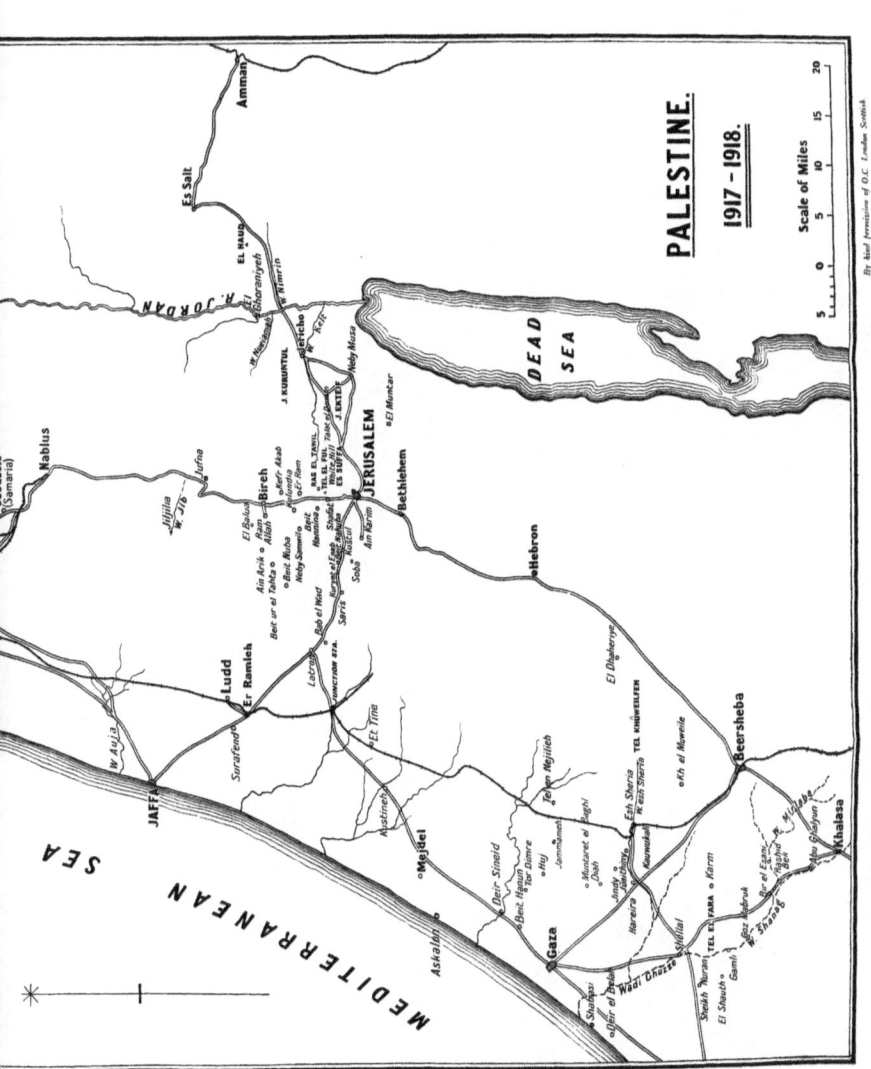

enable wheeled vehicles to be drawn more easily by ponies and mules. Of course the camel was the ideal beast of burden for these conditions, and these animals were there in thousands with their attendant drivers, Arabs, Egyptians and Soudanese. The special virtues of the camel are his suitability for work on soft ground and his capacity for going without water for long periods—but this latter he made up for by drinking an enormous quantity when he got his opportunity.

Belah, the immediate destination of the battalion, was situated only a mile or so from the Mediterranean shore, and offered magnificent facilities for surf-bathing. Needless to say, these were eagerly embraced by the men. In this connection a splendid example of the official lack of any sense of humour was provided by an order issued to the effect that, when troops went bathing in the sea, officers commanding companies were held personally responsible that all dentures were removed before the men entered the water. The inference that even if men were so unfortunate as to get drowned their false teeth (sealed pattern) must be saved, tickled the Cockney humorists not a little.

The operations of the Egyptian Expeditionary Force had begun in 1914 with the repulse of a very determined and well-organised raid by the enemy on the Suez Canal. For the raiders there was no desert railway, no pipe-line, no wire road. They had to travel practically self-contained, as invading armies had done over the same ground, in one direction or the other, for countless centuries down to the time of Napoleon. Little wonder that the effort fell short of success : it says much for the good organisation and determination of the Turks, or their German advisers, that they bombarded the shipping in the Canal with quite heavy artillery, and got it away again. The E.E.F. had also to cope with a serious onslaught from the Senussi in the west, but this also was crushed, though not without difficulty. During the ill-starred Gallipoli Campaign, Egypt was the base from which the operations were conducted, and after its failure there was a good deal of hesitation as to the best use to make of the troops thus released. There was much talk of a landing in the neighbourhood of Alexandretta, at the extreme eastern end of the Mediterranean, with a view to cutting in on the Baghdad Railway. Eventually, however, the troops were dispersed, some to France, some to Salonika, and some to Mesopotamia, while some remained in Egypt to form the nucleus of the force which was to operate against Palestine from the south. Gradually the advance was pushed across the desert, and by the spring of 1917 it had reached the outskirts of Gaza, the gateway to Palestine. The first attack on Gaza all but succeeded, and indeed success might have been complete if the higher command had pushed it with greater determination. But instead a halt was called, and a few weeks later a second attempt was made against the same positions. As these had been much strengthened in the meanwhile, and the new attack lacked the element of surprise, it is hardly astonishing that the result was a complete and costly failure.

Such, in brief, was the position when the 60th Division appeared on the scene, and General Allenby assumed command. There was obviously need for complete change of plan. Before long it began to transpire what that plan was to be, and it also became abundantly clear that no effort was to be spared by the authorities at home to ensure success.

———

CHAPTER VII.

Preparing for the Attack.

For about three weeks, training continued in the Belah district with pleasant interludes for bathing, sports, concerts, and the like, all indicative of the new policy of keeping up the spirits and *morale* of the troops. Some of the senior officers made excursions up to the front line, facing the Gaza defences, and found there a colourable imitation of the trench-war conditions of which we had had experience in France. It was soon obvious, however, that the new G.O.C.-in-Chief had no intention of allowing himself to become involved in the hopeless state of stalemate that had settled on the Western Front, and towards the end of the month the Division began to move away north-eastwards into the desert, roughly in the direction of Beersheba.

The process of reorganisation was going on in all directions. The whole force was divided into two Army Corps and a Cavalry Corps; the former were commanded by Generals Chetwode and Bulfin respectively; and the mounted corps, which was composed of Australians, New Zealanders and English Yeomanry, by General Chauvel. General Bulfin had been in command of the 60th Division since Sutton Veney days, and his promotion was recognised as being in part a tribute to the pitch of efficiency to which the Division had attained under his command. He had come to the Division with rather a ferocious reputation, rumour having it that he had previously had two divisions wiped out. This was probably a picturesque way of saying that he had been involved in some of the fiercest fighting of the early days of the war in France: at all events we found him as reasonable and considerate as circumstances allowed. War at best must always be a beastly and cruel business, and cannot be conducted on the lines of a Sunday School. At all events the divisions were gratified to know that the command of this higher formation was in the hands of a good soldier in whom there was reason to feel complete confidence.

General Bulfin's place as Divisional Commander was taken by Major-General J. S. M. Shea of the Indian Army. Like so many of those who gained distinction in the higher command in the War, General Shea was a cavalryman, and he had commanded the Staff College at Quetta; he was obviously a man of high professional attainments and he was soon to show himself to be possessed of just those qualities of personality which put the men under him on good terms with themselves and one another, and so he got the very best out of them. As his name suggests, he was an Irishman and possessed in a marked degree those engaging characteristics—cynics call them "blarney"—which endear his countrymen to their fellows all over the world. Soon after assuming command of the Division he visited the Senior Officers' School at Heliopolis, near Cairo, and sought out the officers of the Division on the course, none of whom he had met previously. He showed the greatest interest in their welfare, the nature of the instruction, and their personal comfort, and even asked them whether they had enough money! Once when inspecting one of his battalions on parade he found, as not infrequently happened, that one of the platoons was commanded temporarily by a young corporal; he looked the youngster up and down and, turning to the Company Commander, said, "I like that man's eyes, he should be promoted." He had a great weakness for men with red hair, and suggested that a red-headed platoon should be formed in every battalion. It was one of his habits after making an inspection to address the troops; and, doubtless to make it less formal and more friendly, he used to call the men, perhaps a whole brigade of 4,000 or so, to gather round him instead of keeping them formed up in three sides of a square. That of course was quite easily done, but it was another matter when the unfortunate officers and N.C.O.'s had to extricate their men and get them formed up after the pow-wow was over. Perhaps the General wanted to see what sort of a job they would make of it.

The battalion's first move out into the wilderness was to Sheikh Nuran and then to El Sha'uth, nearly twenty miles inland from Belah. El Sha'uth had been carefully prepared for defence by the Turks, but abandoned when they retired northwards across the Wadi Ghuzzee. This outstanding topographical feature was a deep and wide cleft through the sandstone, running north-west past Beersheba to the sea at Gaza. When we saw it first it was almost dry, but the water was not very far below the surface, and it was a very important source of water supply for the Army. The position at El Sha'uth was very strong, and if resolutely held would have been a costly one to capture. Fortunately, however, we were spared that experience. One of the systems of defence consisted of lines of cavalry pits. These pits were eight or ten feet across, six or eight feet deep, and very close together, and as there were about three lines of them it was quite impossible to ride horses across them, and not very easy for a man on foot to get through, especially in the dark. This fact was brought home to a very worthy sergeant of the battalion who, while returning to his lines one night after visiting some posts, had the misfortune to fall into one of the pits, and had to stay there till the morning, when he was able to attract notice to his predicament.

The battalion was nominally in the field, for although the enemy's positions lay some six or seven miles away there were none of our troops in the intervening territory, and of course protective precautions had to be taken. Nevertheless, conditions were not at all uncomfortable. The troops were under bivouacs, but by this time they were quite seasoned campaigners and had learned how to make the best of things. By joining forces eight or ten men were able to contrive quite a good shelter with their sheets and a bit of digging down. The best example of this was provided by the signal section, always a very enterprising and public-spirited unit, who constructed what was known as the Palm Lounge. They had the advantage of access to almost unlimited quantities of wire, and with this and palm and cactus leaves quite an elaborate edifice was constructed, including a "stage" from which very ambitious entertainments were given.

In spite of the great heat and arid nature of the country a good deal of training was done, including some musketry on a range improvised in the desert. Nor was this enough to satisfy the energy of the troops. Football, hockey (in the desert of Sinai in August!) and boxing were enthusiastically indulged in, besides concerts and even a draughts tournament. But by painful experience we began to learn one of the disadvantages of life in such a land as this; every scratch and slight abrasion was apt to turn septic, and the prevalence of the stiff scrub, and especially of cactus such as prickly pear, made it impossible to avoid this danger. Before long there was hardly a man in the battalion who had not had some part of his anatomy swathed in bandages.

It became more and more evident that a new plan of campaign was in prospect. Almost every day strong mounted patrols, sometimes whole regiments, rode away eastwards into the wilderness, but no inkling of the scheme leaked out. The troops before Gaza kept hammering away, the artillery bombardment being supplemented by the fire of warships lying off the coast. Raids were carried out in the approved " western " fashion, but there was no sign of a third assault on the defences of the town. This, indeed, was by now almost impregnable, for the Turk is a fine defensive fighter.

Towards the end of August the battalion moved up to a position in front of Tel-el-Fara, across the Wadi Ghuzzee. The enemy were holding a line of high ground about five or six miles away, running from Beersheba to Gaza. Reconnaissance became more and more searching; infantry officers used to ride out with cavalry patrols towards the enemy positions to get some idea of the lie of the land. On one occasion the Commander-in-Chief himself conducted a reconnaissance in force, driving out with his staff in several cars into no-man's-land with the whole Australian Mounted Division as escort. It was indeed an impressive spectacle.

The battalion and the rest of the division practised attacking under open warfare conditions, sometimes complete with overhead machine-gun fire. The activities of the Air Force were steadily increasing. General Allenby had insisted on being provided with very strong reinforcements in this branch of the service, and soon they established complete superiority in the air and were able to carry out invaluable reconnaissance work. Perhaps the most important problem to be solved in connection with an offensive campaign in a desolate country such as lay before us is that of Supply. The water problem presented enormous difficulties. As has been said, there was always water to be had in the Wadi Ghuzzee ; but how much nobody knew for certain, and what were the resources of the country ahead of us nobody had the least idea. It was fairly certain that we should have to rely on camel transport for nearly everything, ammunition, rations and water included. Thousands and thousands of camels were brought up, organised into companies of about fifteen hundred : it must be remembered that for every two camels there was a native driver, so in themselves they created a new problem in supply for the " Q " Dept.

A branch railway was extended across the Wadi Ghuzzee out into no-man's-land to Karm, and the water resources of the Wadi were exploited to the utmost. The pipe-line from the Nile was doubled and trebled in capacity. It was clear that nothing that could possibly contribute to success was being omitted. Troops were evidently to be used in large numbers far away from the coast sector, but no actual move was made, for in such a *terrain* the clouds of dust raised by marching columns, and by the transport necessary to keep them supplied, would at once have drawn attention to their presence. For the time being, therefore, the 60th Division was left all on its own out in the desert, except for the cover afforded by the mounted units which were continually passing to and from the north-east. During this period a change took place in the command of our 180th Brigade. It was apparently considered that the conditions of the coming campaign would prove too arduous for a man of General Carleton's age, and there were rumours that he was not exactly hitting it off with General Shea. At all events he was succeeded in command of the brigade by General Hill, who in turn, after a very short time, was promoted to command the 52nd Division and succeeded by General C. F. Watson. General Watson was a regular officer of the Queen's Royal West Surrey Regiment and had seen much service and gained distinction in France. He very speedily made his presence felt and was very keen to make the acquaintance of the various units under his command as quickly as he could, thus confirming the impression that great events were imminent.

While all these preparations were afoot there was no change in the policy of allowing as much leave as possible, and of ensuring that the troops were made as comfortable as the conditions allowed. Rations were good, and canteen stores fairly plentiful. Difficulties of transport limited the amount of leave to Egypt, but a very good rest camp was established at El Arish, a pleasant oasis on the coast.

CHAPTER VIII.
BEERSHEBA AND SHERIA.

All through August and September and into October preparations went on. Whether the battalion was " in the line " or back in reserve, training was the main consideration, with intervals for sport and entertainment. Meanwhile, the accumulation of stores and equipment was proceeding on a lavish scale ; especially noteworthy was the additional strength and proportionately greater activity of the air service. It was a rare thing now for an enemy 'plane to come over our lines, but our own machines were constantly making prolonged flights for purposes of reconnaissance mainly over the enemy lines. Considerable reinforcement of heavy artillery (mostly 6-inch howitzers) and mechanical transport was also becoming available. The actual fighting units were strengthened by the arrival of the 10th (Irish) Division from Salonika ; they had been in Gallipoli and Macedonia for more than two years and were much weakened by the ravages of malaria. A new (75th) Division was formed, partly of West Country Territorial units from India and Mesopotamia, and partly of native Indian battalions, with the addition of a regular battalion, the 1st Loyal North Lancs. from East Africa. Early in the year the 74th Division had been formed from dismounted English Yeomanry regiments. The total force consisted therefore of three mounted divisions, viz., Australian, Anzac (Australian, New Zealand and Yeomanry) and English Yeomanry.

BEERSHEBA—TURKISH TRENCHES, HILL 1070.

BRIDGE DESTROYED BY TURKS AT SHERIA.

The force was almost entirely composed of Territorial troops. The infantry divisions were 52nd (Lowland), 53rd (Welsh and Home Counties), 54th (East Anglian), 60th (London), 74th (Dismounted Yeomanry), all territorial, 75th (Mixed), and 10th (Irish New Army). There were in addition various army troops, including a heterogeneous brigade consisting of French, Italian and British West Indies troops, for whom the British Tommies coined the name of " Mixed Vermouth."

No official indication of the plan of campaign was given, but it gradually transpired that under cover of a feint bombardment and demonstration at Gaza the main effort was to be made by the 20th Corps (consisting of 53rd, 60th and 74th Divisions under General Chetwode) at Beersheba, with the bulk of the mounted troops working round on the right of the main attack towards the same point. The primary aim of this movement was to gain possession of the wells of Beersheba, at the head of the Wadi Ghuzzee, which had played an important part in the history of this corner of the world for many thousands of years. In order that secrecy should be preserved as far as possible the 53rd and 74th Divisions were not moved up to the right flank until the very last moment, and the mounted troops were not concentrated in such a way as to indicate to the enemy that the main blow was to be struck so far from the sea. It was hoped, and the hope was realised, that the enemy would think that another and greater push was to be made against the Gaza defences. The whole course of events was such as to fill the Army with confidence that their efforts were to be used to good purpose. The higher commanders did their share, and in our case both General Shea and General Watson did everything possible to maintain the *morale* and confidence of the troops. The dream of Christmas in Jerusalem did not seem quite so impossible of attainment.

Towards the end of October events moved rapidly, and after a couple of night marches the battalion was in its position on the morning of the 31st to take part in the first stage of the great advance. With the cavalry moving round the right flank the 60th Division was on the right of the main attacking force, with the 53rd on the left and the 74th in Corps reserve. The 181st and 179th Brigades made the attack, with our own 180th Brigade in immediate support. The objective was a hill (marked 1070 on the maps) which was strongly held by the Turks to cover Beersheba. The attack was so completely successful that the 180th Brigade never came into action, and by the afternoon the Australian Light Horse were in Beersheba and in possession of the wells. The success of the surprise may be judged by the fact that the enemy had not troubled to destroy, or even damage to any extent, this invaluable source of water supply.

This first operation having proved entirely successful, it was naturally of the greatest interest to know what the next move was to be. Was it intended to advance on Jerusalem by the Beersheba-Hebron-Bethlehem road? Mounted troops were thrown out in that direction, but it was hardly conceivable that the difficulties of transport and water supply for a large force could be faced. Or was the attack on Beersheba merely a feint designed to draw the enemy's reserves off from Gaza, and was the main effort to be renewed there? A heavy bombardment of the Gaza defences had been carried out by sea as well as by land since before the opening of the offensive and it appeared to be growing in intensity. It soon transpired, however, that the plan of campaign was for the 20th Corps, consisting of 10th, 53rd, 60th and 74th Divisions, which had taken the almost isolated position at Beersheba, to wheel to the left and advance in a north-westerly direction against the exposed left flank of the main enemy position at Kauwukah, Sheria and Hareira, with intent to roll up the whole line.

The water difficulty was proving even greater than had been anticipated, although the enemy had done but little damage to the wells at Beersheba. The weather was unusually hot and dry for the time of year, and this of course added to the problem. It was not till the 6th November that any considerable move could be made. On that day the 53rd Division advanced and captured the Khuweilfeh position, about eight miles due north from Beersheba. Meanwhile, the 74th and 60th Divisions, moving north-west, attacked the Kauwukah positions, some ten miles from Beersheba. The 74th on the right met with strong opposition, but succeeded in capturing the Rushdi system of defences before nightfall. The line of approach to the Kauwukah position, the objective of the 60th, was over very broken country, a sandy desert intersected by deep wadis, in crossing which it was a matter of the greatest difficulty to maintain direction. The enemy's artillery barrage was very heavy, and consequently advantage was taken of the wadis as providing cover from both view and fire ; but this still further added to the difficulty of keeping direction and touch with neighbouring units.

The 179th and 180th were the attacking brigades, with the 181st in reserve : 180th had 18th and 19th battalions in the first line, with 20th in support. Major Gray, who was in temporary command of the 19th (Col. Sword having been attached to the divisional staff for the time), went ahead with " A " Company as an advance guard and lost touch with the remainder of the Battalion. The other companies, however, pushed forward on the general line which had been indicated and, with not very heavy casualties, reached their objective by about 4 p.m.

By a strange irony of fate the first man in the Battalion to be hit in the advance and in the campaign, too, was Corporal Plant, the regimental postman, whose job, important and arduous as it was, would have been considered as safe as any in an infantry unit ; he was hit by a splinter from an aeroplane bomb and unfortunately died of his wounds. Lieut. Vincent of " A " Company also was shot through both legs.

The Kauwukah system having been gained, the 20th were pushed on to Sheria station, on the south side of the Wadi, where the Beersheba railway crossed the Wadi Sheria by a lofty viaduct. They succeeded in gaining a footing in the station, but the enemy were in strength on Tel-esh-Sheria on the opposite side of the Wadi, and the 20th were unable to consolidate the position.

The capture of Sheria was a matter of great importance, for it involved the control of considerable sources of the water supply which was the Division's greatest need. The enemy evidently realised that it was impossible for them to stem the advance of our troops, for they took advantage of the temporary check to set fire to their dumps of stores and ammunition and to blow up two spans of the railway viaduct. For the time being, therefore, the troops were almost entirely dependent for water and rations on the camel convoys coming up from Beersheba and Karm respectively. On receipt of news at Corps H.Q. at Beersheba that Sheria was in our hands, early in the afternoon the two convoys set out on their long trek with orders to meet near Irgeig *en route* and dump their loads near the railway station on the banks of the wadi. As has been said, however, we had not been successful in consolidating this position and our outposts were actually some 500 or 600 yards on the near side of the wadi. But such was the confusion of the general situation that this huge convoy of 3,000 camels proceeded right through our positions and even our outposts and in the pitch dark dumped its loads where ordered, several hundred yards out in no-man's-land. The officer conducting the convoy belonged to the 19th and his feelings when he realised that he had jeopardised the essential means of livelihood of the whole of his division may be imagined. When he reported back at Beersheba his statement was received with incredulity by the Deputy Q.M.G. But there was no question about the facts, for the regimental quartermasters could not draw their much-needed rations until the advance had been resumed.

It was not without further heavy fighting that the crossing of the wadi was gained. Very gallant work was done by the artillery, who galloped their guns into action in the open under heavy machine-gun fire from the high ground held by the enemy. They suffered seriously in men and horses. The infantry also lost heavily; Lieut. Ashton, an officer of the Loyal N. Lancs., attached to the 19th, was killed, as also were Capt. Cotton of the 17th, Capt. Harding of the 18th and Capt. Travers of 20th, all old friends and comrades of long standing. Later in the day, when the crossing had been effected, the Brigade Commander called a conference of officers, representing the battalions, on the hill from which the enemy had inflicted such heavy losses upon us. Major Gray represented the 19th, and just as he arrived on the summit he was killed by a bursting shell which also seriously wounded Capt. Crockett, the Brigade Major. The Brigadier himself had a narrow escape.

The death of Major Gray was a sad blow to the battalion. He was attached from the Royal Scots shortly before we left England and very soon settled down as one of the family party. His vivid personality and good heart—combined with a Scottish accent—endeared him to all. In the line in France he was always devising means of annoying the enemy, and he had a sometimes embarrassing passion for bombs large and small. On one occasion a large dud enemy trench-mortar bomb fell on the parapet of our support line, and he displayed a most unhealthy interest in its interior economy. He explained quite clearly to the company commander in whose sector the beastly thing had dropped that a small wheel had become jammed and so the detonation had been delayed; almost immediately the wheel began to revolve and there was no dallying about in that particular traverse during the next few seconds. In Macedonia he was detailed to command the battalion raid—which was eventually cancelled—and the preliminary reconnaissances and preparations gave him ample opportunity to show his ingenuity and resource. It was cruel luck that he should have been knocked out just as he had got the chance to show his mettle in command of the battalion during the advance into Palestine.

The campaign as a whole was working out pretty well to plan. The defeat of the enemy's left flank at Sheria made the right flank untenable and he hurriedly evacuated the strongly fortified positions around Gaza and retreated precipitately. The *rôle* of the 20th Corps was now to push forward in a north-westerly direction and try to cut off the Turks as they retreated northwards. The 60th Division accordingly on the 8th November marched on into an even more arid wilderness than before, the immediate objective being Huj. The Yeomanry Mounted Division were in front of them and on this day the Warwick and Worcester Yeomanry regiments made a most gallant cavalry charge on some Turkish batteries which they captured at the point of the sabre: this was one of the very few episodes in the whole of the Great War when cavalry were able to perform their traditional part.

The water difficulty was becoming more and more acute. The supplies in the wadi at Sheria were not up to expectation, and the country into which we were now moving was almost entirely waterless. Rain was expected daily, but it did not come. From Huj moves were made to the Wadi Jemmameh and subsequently to the Wadi Hesi in the hope of finding water, but with no success in either case. The troops were still almost entirely dependent for water supply on the camel convoys, and their limit of range had been reached. By 15th November, therefore, it was decided that it was no use keeping the Division up in this waterless area any longer. The enemy had retired to Jerusalem or beyond Jaffa, and our troops on the coastal sector—the 21st Corps—were hard on their heels. The 74th Division had already been withdrawn to the neighbourhood of Gaza and the 53rd were covering the Hebron Road. On the 16th November, therefore, the whole 60th Division began to move back to Hareira and roughly along the line of the Turkish defences to Gaza.

The weather continued excessively hot and the marches were very trying, being over very rough ground. Many gruesome relics of the bitter fighting for Gaza in the spring were seen, including an abandoned tank. The battalion reached Gaza on 19th November, and on that day the first rain fell; this of course was a great relief, although it added to the difficulties of wheeled transport. Next day we started northwards again along very fair roads in the wake of the 21st Corps. On 23rd November we reached Latron at the foot of the defile in the road leading up to Jerusalem. We anticipated a period of rest here, but after one day, on 25th, orders were received to move up at an hour's notice to relieve one of the divisions in

SAND CARTS, 2/5TH LONDON FIELD AMBULANCE.

LIGHTLY WOUNDED ON CAMELS.

TWO METHODS OF CONVEYING WOUNDED.

the line which was about five or six miles short of the city.

The first stage was along the main road, through a wonderful rocky defile which looked as though it might have been impregnable if resolutely held, but so precipitate had been the enemy's retreat and so close our pursuit that no organised resistance had been made at all. By about 6 p.m. we had reached Enab, a village with a large monastery some seven or eight miles from Jerusalem. Here a halt was called, and after two or three hours' rest and much issuing of orders and counter-orders, the 180th Brigade moved northwards towards Kubeibeh along what the maps marked as a Roman road. Actually it was the merest track, strewn with enormous boulders which might originally have been the foundations of the road but were now a grave obstruction, especially to wheeled transport and camels. As we picked our way painfully along this travesty of a road we had little reason to think of our proximity to the Holy City until there rang out through the stillness of the night the bell of the monastery at Kubeibeh calling the monks to prayer regardless of the warlike scenes around them. It was uncanny in the extreme to hear this peaceful sound in the midst of our painful and uncertain efforts.

Eventually the 17th and 19th Battalions were pushed up to relieve two battalions of the Scottish Rifles at Nebi Samwil, where very heavy fighting had been going on during the previous week. First the 75th Division and then the 52nd had captured and recaptured this key position, which commanded not only a view of Jerusalem itself, but more important still, the Nablus Road leading northward from the city. It is the reputed burial place of the prophet Samuel, and also the spot from which Richard Cœur de Lion got his only glimpse of Jerusalem.

NEBI SAMWIL—FROM THE TURKISH POSITIONS.

CHAPTER IX.

NEBI SAMWIL.

The position was handed over by the Scotsmen very hurriedly, and no wonder, for it was getting on for dawn and they had a long way to go over the open before they were out of observation. They had themselves taken over from the 75th Division only two days previously and both divisions had had hard fighting and suffered considerable casualties. The 75th, in particular, had taken, lost and retaken the position on successive days.

As day broke the difficulties of the position, which previously had been very vague, became perfectly obvious. Two companies, " D " and " B," were in front line, with the other two and Battalion H.Q. about 300 yards behind. H.Q. occupied a very dark, low-pitched cave. " D " Company, who were in touch with a company of 17th London, occupied part of the mosque buildings which crowned the hill and commanded a wonderful view of the surrounding country. In addition to the mosque, they held some 200 yards of breastworks (or " sangars " as they were called) running to the left northward ; and " B " Company continued this line over more open country, which sloped gradually downwards from the mosque. " D " Company's line ran along the outskirts of a small village which was held by the enemy and in some places was less than thirty yards distant.

The communications between the front line companies and H.Q. were over the rough open hillside and the posts held were varying distances apart. On the night we took over C.Q.M.S. Scott and a runner, when coming up with rations for " D " Company, walked between two of the posts into the enemy's lines, and both men were wounded and taken prisoner. From the mosque Jerusalem was plainly visible about five miles away, and one could not help wondering whether our efforts would succeed where so many through the ages had failed. The view also included stretches of the main road leading northwards from the city, its main road of communication, near which most of the Turkish batteries were sited ; it was not possible, however, to make a very complete survey because enemy snipers in the houses of the village were rather active. For the same reason movement between the posts by day was very restricted.

The first day and night passed without any important incident. There were evident signs of the heavy fighting that had taken place, and a good many dead were buried, including Gurkhas and men of West Country regiments, belonging to the 75th Division, also Scots of 52nd, some Turks and at least one German. There had evidently been hand to hand fighting, for several " kukris," the broad-bladed knives carried by the Gurkhas, were found lying about.

On the morning of 27th November there was some intermittent enemy shelling, and a hundred or more natives, apparently inhabitants of the village, came over into our lines and were of course interned. Early in the afternoon the enemy opened a most intense bombardment of the mosque and the adjoining posts occupied by " D " Company. All communication with H.Q. was very soon broken and very little retaliation was offered by our own artillery; for one thing the rough character of the country made it very difficult to bring up guns of any kind, and much more so to maintain ammunition supply. Furthermore, the country being extremely hilly and broken, our field guns—18 pounders—with their flat trajectory were almost useless and no attempt was made to bring up any of the divisional artillery except the 4·5 inch howitzers, and they were not yet in position. Consequently, the enemy bombardment proceeded almost without interruption, and being concentrated on so small an area from a large number of batteries (mostly 4·2 inch, but some 5·9) its intensity was very severe. It was comparable, according to those with recent experience in France, with a typical Western Front bombardment. The mosque itself received marked attention and came crumbling down in ruins about the heads of 13th and 14th Platoons who were posted in it. A direct hit was registered on the graceful minaret which was an outstanding feature of the building, and it crashed down in a mighty cloud of dust and smoke. The heaviest losses were sustained by 16th Platoon, who had no protection but the flimsy stone sangars.

Gallant and determined efforts were made by the signal section to retain communication between "D" Company and Battalion H.Q., but the line was broken in many places, and was broken afresh as often as it was repaired. Several attempts were made by runners to get through without avail. Pte. Firmage was killed almost before he was clear of H.Q.; but finally Pte. Scammell, the Company Commander's personal runner, managed to reach

Battalion H.Q. with a message reporting the situation. On the return journey to his company, although not a trained signaller he repaired the line single handed and so contributed in no small measure to restoring communication. For this gallant conduct Scammell very deservedly received the D.C.M. Lieut. Ashdown, the signalling officer, had himself worked up the line to Company H.Q. with Privates Pickersgill and Warr, two of his men. Gallant attempts were made to run out lines from Company Headquarters to the mosque, but the wire was literally shelled to pieces several times over. Pte. Pickersgill was wounded and Pte. Warr stunned by shell fire; and in recognition of their joint effort Pickersgill was awarded the Military Medal. Lieut. Ashdown received a bar to his M.C. in respect of the same occasion.

After about an hour and a half's bombardment the enemy barrage was lifted on to the line of approach to Battalion H.Q. from the rear, and the enemy launched an infantry attack through the houses of the village and over the ground on either side. They evidently expected to find our positions abandoned, or that we had sustained such heavy casualties that no effective resistance would be made. On the contrary, all the posts were still strongly held, and the advance was met by a fierce fire at very close range and from the left flank from " B " Company. A platoon from " C " Company, under Sergt. Crump, was sent up to reinforce 16th Platoon who had suffered severely. Lieut. Davies, in command, had been badly hit in the bombardment, but he very gallantly remained with his men, directing and encouraging them until he was hit again and had to be taken back. Unfortunately, this most efficient and popular officer died next day at the clearing station. Sergt. Cheshire, his platoon sergeant, was shot through the head as the attack was made; he had been with the battalion for two and a half years, having joined in April, 1915 as a mere boy, and obtained promotion in the company step by step. Corporal Husk, who had also been a long time with the company, was very badly wounded.

The attack was pressed time after time, but no impression was made on our position. Very valuable support was given by a section of the Trench Mortar (Stokes Gun) Battery, who were posted in the mosque and dropped their shells with great effect among the houses of the village. The 20th Battalion was meanwhile brought up from Brigade Reserve, but their services were not required, for with nightfall the enemy attacks died away. It was subsequently found that he had sustained several hundred casualties in this attack, which was repelled practically by a single company without artillery support. Our casualties, when the intensity of the bombardment is considered, were remarkably light.

After a quiet night and morning it seemed as though another effort was to be made, for the artillery bombardment started again about 2 p.m. But by this time some of our guns were in position and opened fire, with the result that the effort died down.

On the night of the 28th the battalion was relieved by the 20th and went back into reserve, very weary after its experiences. The companies occupied detached bivouac areas near Biddu. H.Q. and " D " Company lay close together, and about midday, while at their meal, they came under heavy artillery fire again, their position being apparently under direct observation. Fortunately the Turk did not get the range at once ; the first shell fell short and the next went over, so that recognising the symptoms—of " bracketing," as the gunners call it—most of the troops were able to get out of the line of fire by scattering on either side. " D " Company had a man killed asleep in his bivouac, and several cases of minor wounds. H.Q. suffered more severely, the signallers coming off worst ; Sergt. Langlois, the Signal Sergeant, who was the life and soul of the section, was hit and so were several of his men. Needless to say H.Q. and " D " Company moved without unnecessary delay into a less conspicuous position about half a mile away alongside " B " Company.

On 30th November General Shea, the Divisional Commander, came up and on parade decorated Capt. F. Ward, O.C. " B " Company, with the Military Cross for consistently good work throughout the campaign, particularly at Kauwukah. Never was decoration more thoroughly earned, for Capt. Ward was ever untiring in his efforts to secure the military points of a situation and never forgot to make the best possible arrangements for the safety and comfort of the troops under him. Lieut. Hearn of 2/20th received the M.C. on the same occasion and the General took the opportunity to congratulate the 19th on their achievements during the previous few weeks and especially on the action at Nebi Samwil.

Photo: F. Vester, American Colony Stores, Jerusalem. World-wide Copyright.

AN INCIDENT IN THE CAPTURE OF JERUSALEM.

Sergeant Sedgewick, "A" Company, 2/19th, and Sergeant Hurcomb, "D" Company, 2/19th (rifle slung), with the Mayor of Jerusalem and flag of truce party, December 9th, 1917. A native holding the improvised flag of truce is seen in the background.

CHAPTER X.

THE CAPTURE OF JERUSALEM.

It was obvious by this time that preparations were being made for the capture of Jerusalem. General Allenby wished to avoid serious fighting in the immediate vicinity of the city, sacred as it was to Christians, Jews and Moslems. Moreover, the capture of Jerusalem itself, although obviously desirable from the point of view of moral effect, was from the military aspect of less importance than the cutting off of the large number of enemy troops within it. It was therefore planned that the 60th and 74th Divisions should respectively attack the defences on the east and north-east of the city and then, if they were successful, work round to the left and endeavour to cut the road which runs northward from Jerusalem to Nablus. At the same time the 53rd Division, which before the attack began was near Hebron in the south, was to come up on the east side of Jerusalem and cut the road to Jericho. If these plans were successful, the Turkish force in Jerusalem, which was already faced by the British on the west and the south, would be cut off on the north and east sides also, and completely bottled up.

Some preliminary movements were necessary before the final dispositions could be made, and as part of these the battalion, on the night of 2nd-3rd December, went from Biddu into the line at a point north-west of Nebi Samwil. But our stay here was brief ; on the evening of the 5th we were relieved by the 25th Royal Welch Fusiliers, of the 74th Division, and moved back to the Jaffa-Jerusalem road at Saris.

On the next day nothing happened. But by the 7th all was ready, and at noon on that day the battalion marched up the Jerusalem road to Enab and there dumped its packs and surplus kit. The weather, which hitherto had been fairly fine, now broke completely. Rain poured down until even the main road became almost impassable for camels : while the unfortunate troops, who were still wearing tropical drill shorts and sun-helmets and had no overcoats, had now left behind them every means of shelter except the ground-sheet that they wore round their shoulders.

Leaving Enab, the battalion trudged through the mud for several miles until they reached the place of assembly near Kustal. Everyone has noted that, wet to the skin and facing the prospect of battle, they sang as they marched. General Shea rode past the column and shouted a few words of cheer: it is a curious sidelight on the hardships of the period that as a reward for success in the coming fight he promised not only rest but vegetables.

By four o'clock the battalion was halted under the olive-trees of Kustal, and a long wait began. Some hung their ground-sheets from the branches of the trees and dodged as best they could the cascades of rain that poured from every fold. Others, lazier or less optimistic, simply sat or lay on the sodden ground with their ground-sheets wrapped round them. The singing and laughter continued, but men's minds became fixed more and more on the persistent rumour that the cooks were coming up to serve a hot meal.

Unfortunately the wet weather, if unpleasant to the troops, was a sheer disaster to the transport camels. Struggling up and down steep slopes, to which under the best of conditions they were unsuited, many of the wretched beasts slipped and fell, broke their legs, and had to be shot. It gradually became clear that the camels could not be got through, and the hot meal had to be abandoned. But Capt. Bleeze and his men were determined not to be entirely beaten. With enormous labour they man-handled a rum issue over several miles of this appalling country and brought it successfully to the cold and rain-soaked troops. Never was a rum issue more useful and more welcome.

It was not until well after midnight that the battalion left Kustal and began to move towards the Wadi Surar and its position of deployment. A thick mist deepened the darkness of the night. In single file, with fixed bayonets, the troops stumbled along over a seemingly trackless ridge of rough ground. They clambered up and down ledges, caught their rifle-butts against boulders and their bayonets among the branches of the olive-trees. Every now and then the thin line would come to a standstill, as some obstacle held up the men in front. Then the obstacle would be cleared, one's dimly seen forerunners would melt away, and one stumbled along after them at full speed, fearful of losing touch not only for oneself but for all the line of men behind.

At last the bottom of the wadi was reached, and ahead could be faintly made out a steep and towering height. This was Deir Yesin, the position to be attacked. To us was allotted the southern portion of the defences on this ridge; to the 2/17th, on our left, the northern part; and to the 2/18th, farther left again, other works known as the Liver and Heart Redoubts. All these positions were not only naturally strong but had been elaborately prepared by the enemy over a period of many months. Trenches had been blasted out of the rock, squared stones were used for revetting, and above all, each post was protected by cross fire from others. The sole weakness of the defence was that the trenches consisted only of a single line; and this failure to develop the system in depth cost the Turks dear.

The difficulties of the descent to the wadi, and the fact that the ground had not been reconnoitred, resulted in the battalion's being somewhat late in reaching the point of deployment. Furthermore, a doubt arose as to whether the hill which appeared to be our objective was actually the objective or not. This point was resolved by Capt. Radcliffe, who made a personal reconnaissance and from the top of the hill in question was able unmistakably to identify the real Deir Yesin beyond. The battalion then deployed and began a stiff climb, with " B " and " C " Companies (under Captains Ward and Williamson) in the front line and " A " and " D " (Lieutenants Elgood and Tabberner) in support.

Although the very steepness of the hill provided a certain amount of cover, the attacking companies came under heavy machine-gun and rifle fire immediately after deployment, and they soon began to suffer casualties. But after a temporary check, due to the difficulty of keeping touch with the troops on the flank, the battalion went on and carried the crest at the point of the bayonet. This done, the village was soon overrun. The Turks, however, fought with great gallantry, one machine-gunner in particular being bayonetted while still serving his gun.

The capture of the village was completed by about 7.0 a.m. The other battalions had achieved their first objectives earlier; red flares had first been seen in the centre and left before six o'clock, and the 2/18th had by now carried the Heart Redoubt and advanced beyond it on the south of the Jaffa-Jerusalem road. By our own success we had completed the first stage of the Brigade's operations and strengthened the position of the 2/17th, whose right flank had been exposed so long as we were unable to come up.

But a check now ensued. Emerging from the farther side of the village, the battalion met with serious opposition from a group of quarries and from the houses of the Syrian Colony near by. A nest of machine-guns held up the advance for the time being. Artillery support was badly needed, and this it was almost impossible for the gunners to give because of the terrible state of the roads and the fact that the tracks down from Kustal were in full view of the enemy. Ultimately, however, the 301st and 302nd Brigades each managed to get a battery across the Wadi Surar, and from positions within rifle-fire of the Turks these batteries opened fire.

All the remainder of the morning, and well into the afternoon, the hold-up continued. Then it was decided to make a strong assault with almost the whole strength of the 2/19th. Aided by flanking operations carried out by the other battalions the 2/19th carried the position with a bayonet charge, made under the eyes of the Corps Commander and General Shea, who were at the latter's look-out at Kustal. This was at 3.40 p.m., and as far as the battalion was concerned it closed the operations for the day. The positions so hardly won were consolidated as far as possible, and upon them the troops spent a cold, wet night.

Considering the strength of the Deir Yesin defences, and the difficulties which had been encountered, the battalion's losses were not very severe. Serious casualties, however, had been sustained among its officers. Capt. Ward, who commanded " B " Company, was killed ; he was a gallant officer much beloved by his men and a very loyal comrade. Lieutenants Tabberner and Bencher, of " D " Company, were both mortally wounded and died within a few hours ; they too lost their lives while bravely leading their men in the assault. In all, the battalion's casualties in killed and wounded exceeded one hundred. Jerusalem had been won, but not without cost.

Jerusalem had been won—for when the morning came it was found that the Turks had faded away. Sergt. Hurcomb of " D " Company and Sergt. Sedgewick of " A " Company were out reconnoitring at about eight o'clock when they encountered a small party of civilians advancing with a white flag. It was the Mayor of Jerusalem, who had come to offer the keys of the city. The offer of surrender was ultimately passed to General Watson, who commanded the 180th Brigade, and through him to Division, Corps, and the Commander-in-Chief. In the meantime, General Watson, followed by the Mayor, rode forward into the city to reassure the people, and thus the commander of our Brigade was the first British soldier to enter Jerusalem.

For some hours the battalion remained on the outskirts, close by the positions which they had occupied the night before. For the time being the cold and miserable weather had ceased with the fighting, and a brilliant sunshine added the last suitable touch to the general atmosphere of gaiety and content. It was a strange scene. The inhabitants of the city had flocked out to meet the troops, and the crowd of Christians, Jews and Arabs mingled their various costumes with the dingy uniforms of our men, on a ground that was still littered with the relics and casualties of battle. Dignified old gentlemen proffered cigarettes, and girls chattered in French and sometimes in English. To troops who had hardly seen a civilian since they left Egypt six months before it seemed that something had really happened at last.

But although the operations, as far as we were concerned, had been held up for a while, the plans of the higher command were not yet completely carried out. The frontal attack had succeeded: it was now necessary to swing to the left and obtain control of the Nablus Road. During the morning, therefore, the 2/20th passed through the 2/19th and advanced in a northerly direction. The

2/19th, now in Brigade Reserve, followed them. Marching into the eastern suburbs of Jerusalem, the battalion, which was now reduced to about 300 men, soon turned and left the city behind. An advance of a mile or two along a stony wadi brought it within sight of Shafat, a village on the Nablus Road a little to the north of Jerusalem.

The 2/20th encountered little or no opposition at Shafat, and pushed on to the road and the top of the ridge. Here, at Tel el Ful, where a heap of stones marks the highest point and the Nablus Road passes out of sight of Jerusalem, they were also successful with little difficulty; and although later in the day an outbreak of machine-gun firing made a further attack necessary, before nightfall these last gains were securely held and the final stage of the battle was over.

We of the 19th had not been needed for these operations. Nevertheless, we prepared for the coming night with much less gaiety than we had displayed earlier in the day. Then the streets and houses of a conquered city lay before us, its citizens welcomed us, the sun shone brilliantly on our moment of victory. Now Jerusalem had vanished again like a mirage; we were opening our bivouac-sheets once more on a stony ridge, remote from cities and civilisation; and, worst of all, the warm sun had been succeeded by cold and cheerless rain. Victory we still had—but we seemed, in spite of it, to be in for a miserable night.

But the word came, and the battalion moved down from the ridge into the village of Shafat. The 20th spent their night without coats or blankets on outpost duty in the rain. But the 19th lay on warm floors, thick with dust, within the sheltering walls of strange Arab houses. They lit fires that nearly choked them with smoke and decided that the promise of the morning had been redeemed.

On the afternoon of the next day—December 10th—the battalion marched back into the city and occupied billets in the northern suburbs. As the column passed through the streets they felt that now at last Jerusalem was indeed captured. The enveloping movement might not have succeeded—the Turks had indeed evaded the net—but the city was ours, and now, for a while, we were going to live in it.

* * * *

The following extract from the official " Brief Record of the Advance of the E.E.F." describes vividly the departure of the Turks from the city they had ruled so long :—

" Towards midnight (of Saturday, December 8th, 1917) the Governor, Izzet Bey, went personally to the telegraph office, discharged the staff, and himself smashed the instruments with a hammer. At 02.00 on Sunday tired Turks began to troop through the Jaffa gate from the west and southwest, and anxious watchers, peering out through the windows of the Grand New Hotel to learn the meaning of the tramping, were cheered by the sullen remark of an officer, ' Gitmaya mejburuz ' (' We've got to go '), and from 02.00 till 07.00 that morning the Turks streamed through and out of the city, which echoed for the last time their shuffling tramp. . . . .

"The Governor was the last civil official to depart. He left in a cart belonging to Mr. Vester, an American resident, from whom he had 'borrowed' a hitherto unrequisitioned cart and team. Before the dawn he hastened down the Jericho road, leaving behind him a letter of surrender, which the Mayor as the sun rose set forth to deliver to the British commander, accompanied by a few frightened policemen holding two tremulous white flags. He walked towards the Lifta Hill and met the first representatives of the British Army on a spot which may be marked in the future with a white stone as the site of a historic episode.

"The last Turkish soldier is said to have left Jerusalem at about 07.00 by the east gate of the city, which is named after St. Stephen, but even later armed stragglers were still trickling along the road just outside the north wall, requisitioning food and water at the point of the bayonet. This is no grievous crime on the part of defeated troops, uncertain of their next meal, but it is recorded as the last kick of the dying Ottoman authority in a city where it had been supreme for four centuries.

"As the Turkish flood finally ebbed away into the shadowy depths of the Valley of Jehoshaphat the townsfolk roused themselves from the lethargy into which hunger and the Turkish police had plunged them and fell upon a variety of buildings, official or requisitioned for official purposes, and looted them, even stripping roofs, doors and floors from the Ottoman barracks next to the Tower of David for firewood. It must be admitted that, as the Government had furnished and maintained itself almost entirely by uncompensated requisitions, the crowd was only trying to indemnify itself. But this disorder ceased as suddenly as it had arisen on the appearance of the British infantry."

CHAPTER XI.

LIFE IN THE CITY.

With the completion of the operations which brought about the fall of Jerusalem, and the withdrawal of the 2/19th into billets within that famous city, the time seems ripe for a halt in the narrative and a brief description of the City itself as the battalion found it.

When it was first rumoured away back in the summer that the Army authorities hoped to take Jerusalem by Christmas, the optimistic suggestion was perhaps not taken very seriously by the rank and file. By bitter experience we had become accustomed to disappointment. Time after time on the Western Front the carefully prepared and much heralded offensives of the Allies had opened with what seemed great successes, only to peter out in an atmosphere of failure and stalemate. The recent experiences of the E.E.F. before Gaza had been of the same discouraging kind, and it is not to be wondered at if the troops in general were a little inclined to be sceptical about the prospect of any really resounding achievement.

But now, in December, the sceptics were confounded. In six short strenuous weeks the British forces had advanced from the scorching desert lands of the Wadi Ghuzzee, over the arid plain of southern Palestine, into the rocky hills of Judæa, and at last through soaking rain and bitter cold to the very gates of Jerusalem itself. In the campaign the 60th Division had made no small name for itself,

BRIG.-GENERAL C. F. WATSON AND MAYOR OF CITY, JAFFA GATE, JERUSALEM, 9/12/17.

and among its battalions the 2/19th had taken their full part. Parched with thirst they had fought in heat and dust at Kauwukeh and Sheria: weary marching had brought them to the hills: at Nebi Samwil they had shown themselves as dogged in defence as they had earlier been eager in attack; and finally they had stormed the precipitous slopes of Deir Yesin in face of fierce opposition from a brave and powerful enemy.

And now on the field of battle the keys of Jerusalem had been offered to two members of the battalion. History and romance had touched us at last. Stormed in its infancy by David, sacked by the Romans when it was already old, captured by the Crusaders, recaptured by Saladin, impregnable to Richard Lionheart, this most famous city had drowsed for five hundred years under the Turks until we came. And now Londoners walked its streets, the men of Somers Town and St. Pancras held their place where Romans and Saracens had been before them, and a new paragraph had been added to the histories of England and of Jerusalem.

To some of the Londoners these words would have seemed, and will still seem, a flight of sentimental and embarrassing heroics. But it can be safely said that even these felt, however obscurely, that the capture of Jerusalem was in some way a great event. Cockney wit and Cockney cynicism were not to be silenced by any occurrence; but the most flippant might have admitted that in their secret hearts they were a little impressed.

The billet in which the battalion took up its quarters on December 10th was a large modern building towards the outskirts of the northern suburbs of the city. It was entered from a courtyard, and on the side facing this yard it was for some undiscovered reason walled almost entirely with glass. This feature, coupled with the fact that all the floors were of stone, made the place a somewhat chilly and uncomfortable home for troops who had neither blankets nor overcoats. Nevertheless, the possession of any billet at all, let alone a civilised building in a city street, seemed an incredible luxury after months of primitive living, and if the billet itself was not enough there was endless interest and amusement outside its doors.

It is true that the suburb in which we found ourselves was hardly the true Jerusalem. Modern and Jewish, it consisted almost entirely of red-tiled stone houses without grandeur or architectural pretensions. The old city, one guessed, was different, but it was hidden from us by its mediæval walls, within whose gates we were not allowed to penetrate. But for the time being we were well content with what we had. The throngs of Jews and Christians who had come out to meet us on the battlefield seemed determined to pursue our acquaintance in the city. When first we came to the billet, to step outside its gate was to lose oneself in a mob of curious spectators, enthusiastic well-wishers, and persons anxious to turn an honest penny. These last proffered flat cakes of coarse bread, small quantities of tiny sweet cakes, dried figs and almonds, and tobacco which they soon learned must be turned into made-up cigarettes if it was to appeal to the British soldiers.

Troops who had long subsisted on a monotonous diet of " bully and biscuits " were not to be deterred from buying all the food they could pay for, even though the prices asked seemed very high. We did not at first realise that under the Turkish *régime* even the necessities of life had become so scarce that the inhabitants of the city were almost within sight of starvation. They could not resist selling to us the bread they so much needed and we could not resist buying it. Before many days had passed the British authorities had to take a hand: the sale of bread and cakes to the troops was forbidden, and a surprising number of military police appeared at every corner to enforce the prohibition. The trays of the street-vendors thereafter were pathetically—if somewhat ludicrously—bare; but illicit bargains in bread were still made in quiet corners.

The battalion's first stay in Jerusalem lasted from the 10th to the 15th of December. On the evening of the first day the commanders of the four battalions dined with the Brigadier to meet General Shea, and the function was of historical importance, because this was the first occasion on which the King's health was formally drunk in the captured city. In brandy, the only liquor that could be obtained, the ceremony was performed; and the guests then drank General Shea's health, and he theirs as the representatives of the Brigade that had received the surrender of Jerusalem.

On the 11th the battalion was called upon to provide a guard of honour for the Commander-in-Chief's ceremonial entry into the city. Ragged and unshaven (for razors had been left with the spare kit before the attack, and had not yet been recovered) the members of the guard were conscious that their appearance contrasted sadly with the splendour of the occasion and the showy uniforms that followed General Allenby's car. But they felt that none had better right than themselves to be there.

A day or two after this our bare and draughty billet was exchanged for others which were not only more comfortable but nearer to the heart of the city. The battalion was split up among three adjacent buildings, the Lady Evelina de Rothschild's School for Girls, the Church Missionary Society representative's house, and a third building that lay at the back of the school. We were now within a short walk of the city post-office and the main street, the Jaffa Gate though still impenetrable was within easy reach, and the best shops that Jerusalem at that date could muster soon became a familiar haunt of the troops.

As for the billets themselves, they approximated much more nearly than their predecessor had done to our notions of what a city residence should be. The C.M.S. house in particular still retained a great deal of the furniture of an ordinary English dwelling house. Although the house was crammed with troops, who slept on the floor and cooked in the garden, it was still possible—at any rate for a signaller on duty in the missionary's study—to imagine that at any moment the real owners might appear in the doorway and invite one to tea. The other two buildings, being more in the nature of "institutions," were less liable to provoke attacks of home sickness; but the battalion as a whole felt that it was long since they had lived in so civilised and "civilian" an atmosphere.

By the time the order came which broke up this

idyll and sent the battalion back to chilly bivouacs on wet and stony hills, the troops had been thoroughly refitted. Baths had been installed by the R.E.'s at a spot known (if one's memory serves) as Abram's Vineyard, the men were washed and disinfected and new clothing had been issued. All this was almost immediately nullified by the mud of Tel el Ful, and we soon began to wonder whether the comforts of Jerusalem were anything more than a dream.

But the history of the battalion's stay at Tel el Ful will be told in the next chapter. Jerusalem and the front line, though only two or three miles apart, were in different worlds to us. All that need be said here is that on Christmas Eve the battalion, unexpectedly relieved in the line, returned to its billets in the city. Lucky though we were to be able to spend Christmas in Jerusalem, circumstances prevented us from celebrating the occasion as elaborately as we wished. It was known that the Turks were about to make a strenuous attempt to recapture the city; their attack was expected almost hourly; and the battalion, which with the rest of the Brigade was in divisional reserve, had to be ready to move out at the shortest notice. The troops were practically confined to their billets and the mules stood saddled in the courtyard. Nevertheless, and in spite of the fact that rations were short and other articles of food almost unobtainable, Christmas Day was made as festive as possible and a concert was held in the evening.

This stay in the city lasted precariously until December 27th. The battalion returned to Jerusalem once more on January 16th, occupying the same billets as before, and remained there for ten days. By this time, more than a month after its capture, the city had begun to settle down. If, on the one hand, regulations, and military police to enforce them, seemed to have multiplied painfully, on the other hand the attractions which the city could offer had also somewhat increased. The shops, though still poor, were no longer almost destitute of goods, and it was even possible for the troops to choose between two or three little restaurants where, openly and legally, they were offered half a dozen tiny cubes of cooked meat as a meal.

It must have been at this period that the Divisional Concert Party, which under the name of the Roosters earned lasting fame during the campaign and afterwards, arrived in Jerusalem and opened their Christmas season in a room opposite the Jaffa Gate. Their difficulties must have been enormous, but the show they produced, ending in a potted pantomime called " Cinderella, or the Army Boot," was an ingenious and witty triumph which their comrades in the battalions admired and greatly enjoyed. Life in Jerusalem was becoming more civilised than ever.

All this time the Old City remained, as far as our daily life was concerned, cut off and unexplored. Indian sentries still stood before its gates, and we, when we reached the threshold, could only turn aside. But although the ban continued it was now lightened to the extent that Army chaplains were permitted to conduct parties, of manageable size and under strict supervision, on a tour of inspection of the famous sites and buildings within the walls.

There was much competition for admission to these parties, and it is safe to say that although most men were able to make only one hasty and restricted visit the impressions gained from it became a very vivid and cherished memory. It seems worth while to attempt to record some of these impressions, lest in the passage of years they should fade.

The party would go in by the Jaffa Gate, or rather by the wide breach alongside it which was made for the triumphal entry of the Kaiser in 1898, and in 1917 was not yet closed up. Inside the walls we saw that the carriage road continued for a hundred yards or so and then narrowed itself into a steep and oriental alley which was in fact the main shopping street of the real Jerusalem. But the party did not enter David Street, it turned to the right, passing the main front of the Tower of David, the picturesque mediæval fortress whose foundations date at least from Herod's day. Soon we were in a lane, no wider than David Street but much quieter. The high walls of Armenian monasteries ran on either side, there were glimpses of gardens, and now and then the black-robed figure of a monk or priest would slip noiselessly past. The lane was a long one, leading right up to the south wall of the city. Soon the party had passed through the Zion Gate and were making their way through a medley of narrow turnings outside. These brought us to the Cœnaculum, a room adorned with ancient pillars, which in Christian tradition is the Room of the Last Supper. The Moslems believe that the tomb of David is in the same building, and for centuries have retained the site in their possession.

Re-entering the walled city by the Zion Gate, or perhaps by the small Dung Gate farther east, we find ourselves after some windings in a narrow, open space which is hemmed in on one side by a great wall of huge squared stones. This is the side of the Temple Platform, and this spot is the Wailing Place. Here Jews mourn the decay of their kingdom and the loss of their Holy Places. But we soon leave them, and through one of its gates we pass into the Temple Area itself. It is one of the lovely places of the world. A wide, open space, most of it paved with stones that are dazzling white in the sunshine; a line of old mellow buildings fringing it; tall slender minarets at corners; on the south side the mosque of el Aksa, which some say was once the Templars' church; and in the middle, flanked by delicate arcades, the Dome of the Rock. This central shrine, which so impressed the Crusaders that they built churches of its shape in their own countries long after, has the exterior of its walls covered with coloured tiles of great beauty. Its windows are mosaics of rich glass and its dome has the lightness and grace of perfect planning.

But we in 1918 were not allowed to enter the shrine; we turned away and mounted the battlements on the east side. Below us was the valley of Jehoshaphat, with Absalom's Tomb and innumerable Jewish graves. Beyond the valley stood the Mount of Olives, and on the lower slopes we could see the golden cupolas of the Russian Church and a small walled garden which they said was Gethsemane.

The north gate of the Temple Area led out into narrow streets again. We walked up the Via

Dolorosa, under the Ecce Homo Arch. The streets became narrower, often they were arched over, sometimes they were mere flights of worn, steep steps. We came out at last into a small courtyard, surrounded by buildings. One of them, with a tower and a small dome and much worn carving on its stones, was pointed out to us. It was the Church of the Holy Sepulchre, the place where, as for many centuries countless Christians have believed, stood Calvary and the Tomb of Christ. This was the climax of our pilgrimage—for here again we were not allowed to go inside.

And here we may leave Jerusalem. The battalion was to return more than once to the surrounding hills, where they could sit in their bivouacs and survey the whole city, the walls, the Dome of the Rock, the churches and the minarets. But they were never again to live in its streets. Their billets knew them no more.

CHAPTER XII.

The Defence of Jerusalem.

On the 15th December, at the end of its first stay in billets in Jerusalem, the battalion moved out on to the northern ridge, near Shafat, and took up a position in support of the London Irish. Four days later we relieved them in the line. The defences here consisted of stone *sangars* which were held only at night; in the daytime we withdrew to the nearer slope of the hill. The weather was very wet and cold.

On the 23rd the London Irish, with the 2/19th in support, made an attack on Khurbet Adaseh, a strongly held ridge which was opposite to our part of the line. The operation was intended as a preliminary to an advance on a much larger scale, which the General Staff hoped would push the whole line several miles farther from Jerusalem and so render the city more secure from recapture. Unfortunately the 2/18th's attack, though made with the greatest gallantry, was not a success: it was brought to a standstill by severe fire from the Turks and had at last to be abandoned. The casualties suffered by the London Irish were very heavy; and our own battalion, through whose lines the disastrous attempt had been made, shared fully in the sadness of its comrades' loss.

An officer of the 2/19th who went out with a party, after the attack had been called off, to assist in bringing in the wounded, records that although

JERUSALEM, LOOKING TOWARDS THE MOUNT OF OLIVES.

the party used electric torches freely the Turks did not fire or molest them in any way. He saw no indication that the British dead had been ill-treated, except to the extent that the Turks, perhaps not inexcusably in view of their own privations, had robbed them of clothing and boots.

Extremely bad weather now made it necessary that the proposed general offensive should be postponed, and the plans of the higher command were still further modified by information that the long-anticipated enemy counter-attack, aiming at the recovery of Jerusalem, might be expected immediately. As a direct consequence of the altered plans, the 180th Brigade was relieved in the line by the 179th on December 24th, and thus the battalion was enabled to spend Christmas Day in Jerusalem.

The enemy attack was expected almost hourly. But Christmas Day passed without incident; and on Boxing Day, although the 2/20th received orders to move out of the city and form a reserve for the 181st Brigade, the remainder of the 180th still continued in their billets. That same evening the Turkish onslaught came.

The main attack, which began soon after 1.0 a.m. on the 27th, was made on both sides of the Nablus Road, and was thus largely borne by the 179th Brigade, to whom we had handed over three days earlier. The enemy's choice of this area was dictated by the fact that, although in the immediate neighbourhood of Jerusalem the ground on the northern side is as broken and difficult as it is elsewhere, there is here, some distance back, a fairly level ridge on which troops can deploy and move in open formations.

As a preliminary an outpost of the 2/16th London was driven off Ras el Tawil, east of the road, while the posts held by the 2/13th on the road itself were also forced to withdraw. The attack on the main defences followed. Rushing forward with bombs, the Turks succeeded in effecting a lodgment in part of the 2/13th position, from which they were driven out with the bayonet a few minutes later. At the other points in the sector the enemy attack was completely repulsed by rifle and machine-gun fire, aided by the artillery barrage, which came down very promptly. The enemy then withdrew slightly to reorganise.

In their attack on Tel el Ful, just east of the Nablus Road, the Turks were more successful. After a heavy bombardment they captured the hill at about 3 a.m., and some two and a half hours later a second attack, farther east, resulted in their gaining the whole of the 2/16th's front line position. The 2/13th, who hitherto had been able to hold their ground, suffered so severely from machine-gun fire from Tel el Ful, as well as from enemy shrapnel, that at 6.30 a.m. they had to fall back a couple of hundred yards.

One company of the 2/15th was now gradually drawn in to strengthen the defence. A second company, attached to the 2/16th, counter-attacked on the enemy's right flank. But although the Turks were temporarily dislodged the attackers had ultimately to withdraw after suffering heavy losses.

During the morning there was a lull, which enabled our troops to reorganise and strengthen their position. But before 1.0 p.m. the Turks launched a violent attack on the 2/13th from behind the ridge north-east of Beit Hannina. The front line trenches were temporarily lost, but within an hour the 13th and a company of the 15th charged across the crest of the ridge. At the sight of them the Turks fled; and they made no more attacks on this part of the line.

On the left the 181st Brigade had their share of the fighting. In their case the attack opened with an assault at 2.30 a.m. on the 2/24th London on the ridge between Wadi ed Dumm and Wadi Beit Hannina. It was repulsed, and three subsequent attacks, made in great force and supported by heavy artillery and machine-gun fire, were equally unsuccessful. But the progress of the enemy against 179th Brigade, limited though this progress was, made the 2/24th's position untenable, and their line was withdrawn to the nearer slope of the ridge.

The Turks made no further efforts, and by 6 p.m. their activity had ceased on the whole divisional front. Tel el Ful, their only positive gain, was soon afterwards reconnoitred by patrols of the 2/16th and found to be unoccupied. The great attack had been defeated, and that without calling upon any of the reserve battalions, which for the most part were still in billets.

In the meantime events had occurred elsewhere. The 53rd Division, holding the eastern portion of the line, from the neighbourhood of Bethlehem to the Mount of Olives, had, like us, sustained a heavy attack and beaten it off. But to the westward, on our left, the boot had been on the other foot and the

74th Division, attacking instead of defending, had successfully advanced and prepared the way for a general Turkish discomfiture.

On the morning of the 28th, therefore, it became clear that, far from renewing their attack, the enemy had passed to the defensive. The 179th Brigade, which was still in the line, were able during the day to occupy Ras el Tawil and Khurbet Adaseh, the latter with little opposition.

It was now the turn of our own battalion, which, in common with the 2/17th and 2/18th, had remained in billets in the city while the Turkish attacks were being made, but had been brought forward to the vicinity of Shafat during the afternoon of the 28th. In the evening, after Khurbet Adaseh had been taken, the Brigade relieved the 179th, which by this time well deserved a rest, and continued the advance northward. While the 2/20th, on our right, captured the village of Er Ram without great difficulty, we on our side, meeting with even less opposition than they did, easily secured our objective—Brown Hill—before nightfall.

Early in the morning the advance was continued, and the battalion occupied a hill called Tel el Nasbeh. Up to this stage the only serious obstacle encountered was the steep and rocky nature of the country, which grew wilder and more difficult as we went on. But beyond Tel el Nasbeh our advance was held up by artillery fire from the Turkish position at Bireh, and until, in the early afternoon, our own guns came up further progress was delayed. Moving forward then, through a narrow defile, we saw on the skyline a long ridge on which were clearly visible two villages side by side. The one on the right was Bireh, whence came the shells that had delayed our advance, and the one on the left, where red roofs and large buildings seemed to denote a more flourishing and less oriental community, was Ram Allah, the seat of an American mission and the traditional scene where, a day's march out of Jerusalem, the boy Christ was lost and found again by his parents.

But in front of Bireh there stretched forward a huge forbidding bluff. This hill was Shab Saleh: it was occupied by the Turks and until they were dislodged there was little prospect of our reaching the villages. "A" and "B" Companies of the battalion, together with two companies of the 2/20th, advanced to the attack at about 2.30 p.m. They had to descend over broken and difficult ground into a deep wadi and then climb the steep terraced slopes of Shab Saleh for a thousand feet before they came to the enemy's positions. It seemed as if in such circumstances the task of dislodging the Turks was an almost impossible one; but, as in the attack on the Jerusalem defences three weeks earlier, the very steepness of the slope gave our troops a certain amount of cover and enabled them to reorganise before the final rush. The enemy were driven from their *sangars;* they counter-attacked without success and then, with the bayonet, they were forced off the ridge and Shab Saleh was ours. The operation was distinguished by a very gallant feat performed by Sergt. Fry of "A" Company, who single-handed attacked and silenced an enemy machine-gun and earned the D.C.M. This brave N.C.O. was killed in the course of the Second Jordan action, a few months later.

The battalion's casualties in the fight for Shab Saleh were surprisingly light, but during the day they suffered the loss of Lieut. Carey, a valuable officer who had been temporarily attached to Brigade as Intelligence Officer, and was killed by a chance shell-burst while he watched his own battalion going into action.

In the evening the London Irish, with our " D " Company in support, passed through our lines and advanced to occupy high ground on the east of Bireh. The village itself was captured by 181st Brigade. At 9.30 p.m. the line of this brigade and our own went forward once more. On the 180th Brigade front, indeed, the advance continued all night, and Beitin, the ancient Bethel, which lies two miles north-east of Bireh, was taken at 4.30 a.m. on the following morning (December 30th). Although little opposition was encountered, this night march was a fine achievement, for it was made by compass across a series of steep and rocky ravines by troops who carried their own Lewis guns and ammunition.

So ended an operation which, beginning with the repulse of a fierce and powerful enemy offensive, was transformed into a victorious advance that finally and completely confirmed our hold on Jerusalem. Before the advance began the line had been almost within sight and sound of the city: when it closed the two were separated by eight miles, and the Turks had been weakened and demoralised by the total failure of their most cherished hopes.

After the battle was over the battalion remained for some days on the top of Shab Saleh. The weather became increasingly wet and cold, and the troops, living as they did in flimsy bivouacs on this lofty and exposed ridge, might have been excused if they had felt extremely miserable. Moreover, the position of the camp was most inconvenient for transport; in spite of the best efforts of the Quartermaster, rations had to be unloaded some distance from the summit and then carried by hand, with the greatest difficulty, up a series of rock terraces, the walls of which in many places were sheer to a height of twelve or fifteen feet. Altogether there was general satisfaction when on January 3rd the battalion received orders to march back towards Jerusalem and pitch its camp in the neighbourhood of Er Ram.

The day before this move took place Col. Sword was evacuated to hospital and command of the battalion devolved temporarily on Captain Tennant of " A " Company. We did not then realise that the C.O. would never return to us. During the months of hardship and danger through which we had passed since the winter's campaign began Col. Sword had come more and more to hold a vital place in the life and affections of the 2/19th. He was *our* C.O. in a way and to an extent that no successor, however able and popular, could hope to be. It was well, perhaps, for the battalion that they only gradually realised, during the ensuing months, that he would never come back.

Er Ram, the battalion's new station, lies just off the Nablus Road about midway between Bireh and Shafat. It is a picturesque medley of white stone houses, set, like all villages in this part of the country, on the crest of a hill. Headquarters and two of the companies set up their bivouacs on the slopes below the village, but " A " and " C " Companies, under Lieut. Templeton and Capt. Radcliffe respectively, were some distance eastwards, near the village of Jeba. Here they held the line, which on this side ran almost north and south, parallel to, but at a safe distance from, the important Nablus Road.

The weather continued cold and became wetter than ever. It was therefore with great pleasure that the troops received permission to give up their inadequate bivouacs and take up quarters in the deserted village. By European standards the houses of Er Ram might be queerly planned—it was indeed difficult to make out where one dwelling ended and another began, and the front doors of some houses seemed only accessible from the roofs of others—but their solid stone walls were an admirable protection against the icy rain, and their earthen floors had long since been pulverised to a fine dust that made a comfortable bed if not a clean one.

But the rains not only made bivouacs untenable, they seriously interfered with the food supply. The Turkish railway which ran from Gaza and, joining at Junction station the line from Jaffa, curved its way through the Judæan hills to Jerusalem, was at its best hardly sufficient to carry the requirements in rations and stores of all the units which were now in the Jerusalem area. And while we were at Er Ram the transport situation was further complicated by the excessive rains, which not only washed away railway embankments on the coastal plain but also made nearly impassable the road from Hebron, along which, as we understood, the rations of the 60th Division were being brought up in order to relieve the congestion on the railway. At all events, the daily allowance of bully and biscuits, though it never entirely failed, was often skimpy to a degree rarely experienced by the British Army. But this state of affairs was of brief duration. The exertions of the supply services, aided perhaps by the gradual improvement in the weather as the month passed, soon remedied a shortage which was never very serious.

The battalion remained at Er Ram for nearly a fortnight. Within a few days of its arrival the enemy made an attack on Jeba which, although it was easily defeated, cost our " C " Company four casualties. No other event of importance occurred; the fighting that had culminated in the capture of Jerusalem and its subsequent defence against counter-attack had now finally died down. The lull was soon to be brought to an end by operations which would extend in an easterly direction the conquests already made. But this was still hidden in the future; and when, on January 16th, we were relieved at Er Ram by the 2/21st Londons, we moved back to billets in Jerusalem for a brief period of rest and refitting.

CHAPTER XIII.

Talat ed Dumm.

Successful though the Jerusalem operations had been, they had not achieved the object of cutting off the retreat of the Turks, the greater part of whose troops had now withdrawn to the eastward, where the Hedjaz Railway would provide them with lines of communication. The presence of so large a force on the flank of the British army necessarily affected General Allenby's plans for the continuation of the campaign. At first it was proposed to deal with the situation by combining an attack in the Jericho direction with a further advance to the north, but it soon became clear that before the northerly advance could be resumed much time would have to be spent in improving the roads and accumulating stores and supplies. The plan for a simultaneous attack in the east and the north was therefore dropped and preparations directed towards an advance to the Jordan Valley only.

In conformity with this decision, the 60th Division began towards the end of January to relieve the 53rd in the neighbourhood of the Jericho Road, on a line running roughly north and south about three miles to the east of Jerusalem. The 2/19th came out of its billets in the city on January 26th, taking up its position in the line beyond the Mount of Olives, with "C" Company (Captain Radcliffe) on the right at White Hill,

"B" COMPANY, TALAT ED DUMM.

TALAT ED DUMM—THE JERICHO ROAD LOOKING EAST.

"D" Company (Captain Ashdown) at Suffa in the centre, and "B" on the left on another spur. "A" Company, under Captain Tennant, was in reserve, while Battalion Headquarters were in a cave in a wadi off the track that led back to Jerusalem. Here we remained for several weeks.

The weather continued to be very bad, especially at first; and the great rocky hills on which the battalion found itself provided little shelter and no amenities. It was indeed the edge of the wilderness. From the crests of Suffa and White Hill, where rough *sangars* of loose stones formed, with a little wire, the only defences, a bewildering tangle of hills and valleys could be seen stretching away in a declining succession until, in the far distance, they came to an end dimly with the bottomless rift of the Jordan Valley and the blue wall of the Moabite mountains beyond it. Midway in this landscape stood out the central ridge of Talat ed Dumm, where the Jericho Road rose in plain view to a *khan* called the Good Samaritan's Inn, and then passed finally out of sight. This ridge was the main line of the enemy's defences; on any clear day men and horses could be seen there, passing along the dusty white road—just as at Arak Ibrahim, an advance position to the left of Talat ed Dumm and much nearer, one could usually discern the grey form of a sentry at the mouth of Abraham's Cave. The battalion was to become much more closely acquainted with these hills when the offensive had begun.

Towards this coming offensive all our activities were directed. Patrols were sent out by day and by night. It was an exhausting as well as a nerve-racking business, for a patrol would spend nearly an hour at the outset clambering down the rocky slope to the bottom of the wadi beneath and then up the opposite side. Fortunately, the Turks seldom ventured very far afield; and small parties of our men were able more than once to penetrate as far as " Cistern Bend " and up the hill beyond it to a point where they had an excellent view of Abraham's Caves. In addition to the patrolling, posts had to be pushed out at night a long way forward so that they could watch the cavernous depths of the wadis; and communication between these outlying posts and the main position on the hilltop was highly precarious. Nevertheless, a company commander records the fact that, worn out as the men were by atrocious weather, constant patrolling and heavy work on the defences, they remained unaccountably cheerful. But this, as he says, was no unusual phenomenon.

On February 14th the 181st Brigade assaulted and captured the village of Mukhmas. Not for the first time history was repeating itself; for Michmash, at the head of the gorge leading up from Ai and Jericho, was no stranger to warlike affrays in the days of the Old Testament. The Crusaders, moreover, knew it well: and now, once more, its capture was a move in the war-game. But it was not until five days after Mukhmas fell that the offensive we were waiting for really began.

At dawn on the 19th the battalion moved forward. The 180th Brigade was astride the Jericho Road, with the 179th on their right and the 181st on their left. Beyond the 179th Brigade moved the 1st Australian Light Horse and the

New Zealand Mounted Rifles, ready to execute a flanking movement round the Turkish positions and then up the Jordan Valley from the south. On the left of our 181st Brigade the 53rd Division had their part.

Our own battalion was acting in support of the 2/20th, whose orders were to assault the Arak Ibrahim position and the high ground beyond it. The 20th captured Arak Ibrahim itself early in the morning, but were held up on reaching open ground on the farther side of the ridge. Artillery support could only be provided with great difficulty, for the enemy had blown up bridges and guns had to be manhandled up and down the sides of wadis. But the gunners triumphed over all obstacles and during the afternoon the 20th completed their task. In the meantime the 181st Brigade had encountered serious resistance as well as very formidable natural obstacles. Nevertheless, they also were successful in reaching their objectives; and as a result of the day's operations the Division advanced its front an average distance of three miles, while the mounted brigades on the right arrived at El Muntar, only seven miles from the Dead Sea.

The 2/19th had moved forward during the day without meeting much opposition. At "Cistern Bend," however, they were shelled, "B" Company and the Transport being the chief sufferers. Here Second-Lieut. Hood was killed by a direct hit from a "dud" shell which would doubtless have caused many additional casualties if it had exploded.

The night was quiet but at daybreak the next morning (February 20th) the attack was resumed. The 180th Brigade, with the 2/19th in the centre, were now operating against Talat ed Dumm, the commanding eminence that had so often focussed our eyes during the preceding weeks at Suffa. The position was found to be strongly held: but after a heavy bombardment our attacking companies, "A" and "D," went forward with great dash across the open ground at the foot of the hill and up the steep slopes of the hill itself. Capt. Tennant, commanding "A" Company, and Lieut. Gardiner of "D" were both very seriously wounded, and the latter died of his injuries later. But by 7.15 a.m. Talat ed Dumm was in our hands. The hill beyond it was taken soon afterwards and later in the morning, when the troops had reorganized, a successful assault was made on Chastel Rouge. This last-named position takes its name from the Crusaders' fortress which stands, a heap of ruins, on its summit. One may imagine the shades of its bygone defenders looking on with astonishment while high explosive burst on their familiar green slopes and Turkish machine-guns spat death from among the mediæval stones.

While we fought for Talat ed Dumm, the 179th Brigade, on the right of 180th, was attacking Jebel Ektief. The difficulties were great and progress at first was slow. But when Talat ed Dumm had fallen the 2/18th and a battery of guns were able to co-operate with the other brigade, and after very gallant fighting the hill was captured at about midday. In the meantime, the 181st Brigade on the left had also met with considerable difficulty, as much from the nature of the country as from the resistance of the enemy. By nightfall, however, the Division as a whole had advanced another three miles and was now ready to move on its final objective, the hills overlooking the Jordan Plain.

The battalion spent a miserable night in a wadi a mile or two east of Talat ed Dumm. It was bitterly cold, storms of rain were not lacking, and the troops had no other shelter than that provided by a single blanket apiece. But when the morning came the advance was continued in warm sunshine and without hindrance from the enemy. At Nebi Musa, the famous shrine where Mohammedans believe Moses to be buried, the London Scottish occupied without opposition a point from which heavy firing had held up the advance of the New Zealanders on the previous day; the Australians, who had already reached the shores of the Dead Sea, now swept rapidly up the valley and were in Jericho by 8.20 a.m.; and, in short, it was evident that the Turks had retired along their whole line and were now safely on the farther side of Jordan. The 60th Division, therefore, was able to push on without incident down the steep and rocky Old Jericho Road until at last they took up their positions at Khan Khakun, the final objective laid down for them.

From these last hills of the wilderness the whole of the Jordan Valley could be seen laid out like a map. The Dead Sea gleamed in the south, then came the flat plain dotted with sparse bushes. Farther north a patch of luxuriant green, out of which peeped a few miserable houses, indicated Jericho, and across the middle distance ran a thin line of sandhills, showing a hint of vivid green here and there in their midst—the line of the River

Jordan itself. Beyond the Jordan the plain went on until at last it was hemmed in by hills as high and steep as those we came from. These were the Mountains of Moab. Es Salt and Amman lay hidden in these hills : but as yet their names meant nothing to us. It was just unknown enemy country.

A few officers and men were able to visit Jericho, and many more inspected, now or later, the strange Greek Monastery of St. Nicholas, whose façade of masonry clings half-way up a sheer cliff in the side of the Wadi Kelt. But only a day or so was spent at Khan Khakun. The battle was over and the 19th were soon withdrawn to camp on a hillside just below Talat ed Dumm. Here the Inn of the Good Samaritan and the ruined pile of Chastel Rouge stood to remind us of the battalion's latest achievement ; and along the road, beside our bivouacs, an everchanging procession of troops, military vehicles, Palestinian families on foot and on donkeys, and sometimes even a dilapidated cab from Jerusalem, helped to lessen the monotony that began now to be increasingly felt. For we were to remain at Talat ed Dumm for several weeks, attending to those tasks which are believed to improve the discipline and morale of the soldier.

In the meantime the high command was contemplating an operation against the Turks on the farther side of Jordan. For this purpose there was constituted a force known as "Shea's Group," after the G.O.C. 60th Division, who was in command of it. The force consisted of the Australian and New Zealand Mounted Division, the 60th (London) Division, the Imperial Camel Corps Brigade, a heavy battery, the 6th Mountain Artillery

Brigade, a light armoured-car brigade, and two bridging trains. The inclusion of the last-named served as an indication that one of the first and most difficult of the tasks to be faced in this new project would be the crossing of the Jordan, which in the spring of the year is in flood.

CHAPTER XIV.
THE FIRST JORDAN RAID.

Before the raids could be undertaken it was first of all necessary to reconnoitre as thoroughly as possible the territory between our positions near Talat ed Dumm and the Jordan, and particularly the banks of the river itself. This was a task of considerable difficulty, mainly on account of the nature of the country. The terrain is one of the most extraordinary in the world, for the river flows at a level over a thousand feet below the sea, while the hills east of Jerusalem are nearly 3,000 feet above sea-level, and this drop occurs within a distance of not more than fifteen miles. The country is extremely bare and rugged and is cut across by steep valleys running down to the river from west to east, so that communication north and south is almost impossible. Through this unfriendly land, therefore, the troops marched out day after day to explore the approaches and crossings of the Jordan. The river was found to be in full flood and flowing very fast, and the alleged fords quite impassable. Even at this early season the heat in the river valley was found to be very intense.

Besides the duty of reconnaissance an enormous amount of work had to be put in at constructing and improving roads, and the bulk of this, as ever, fell upon the long-suffering infantry. But it must not be thought that our wonderful Cockneys were at all worn out by the rigorous compaigning in these

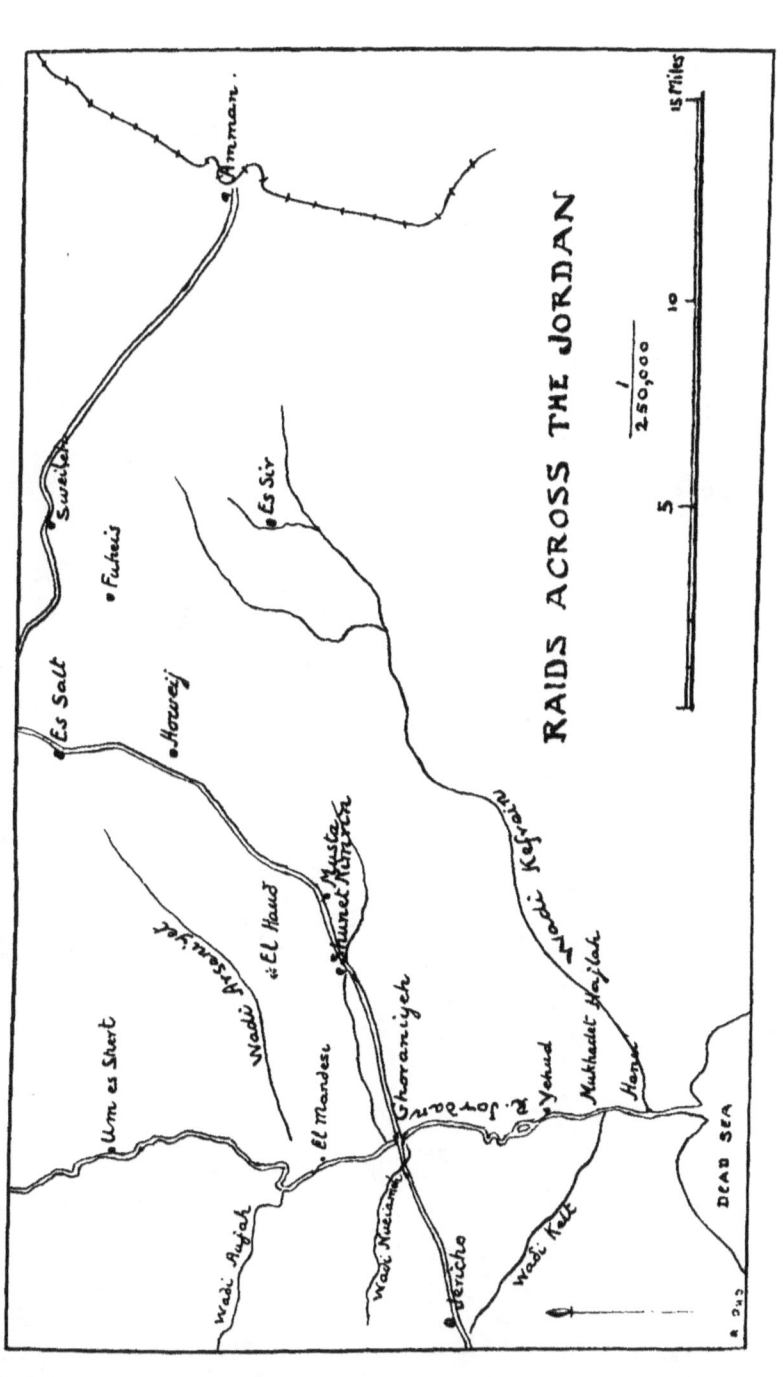

trying conditions, for during the comparative calm of this period of preparation a series of inter-platoon, inter-company, and inter-battalion football matches was carried through, and in spite of the rocky and hilly nature of the ground they were keenly contested and much enjoyed. The two divisional concert parties, the Barnstormers and the Roosters, also contributed their quota to keeping up the spirits and morale of the troops.

The strategic influence of the intended raid was widespread. The enemy, of course, were not long ignorant of what was in prospect, but the project also involved an area extending to the Arab kingdom of Hedjaz and to Mesopotamia, and even caused a fluttering in the dovecotes at German Headquarters, where the greatest importance was attached to the position in the Middle East. The effect on the local tactical situation was to leave the enemy in doubt whether Allenby's objective was to advance northward along the coast line or to join hands with the Emir Feisul and advance on the east side of the Jordan.

The work of reconnaissance culminated on 4th March, when the whole battalion moved off from Talat ed Dumm towards the river in an effort to locate the fords which were reputed to exist in the neighbourhood of El Ghoraniyeh. Headquarters were established at the Blue Dome Monastery, the monks of which seemed utterly bewildered at the sudden invasion of their privacy; although to some it seemed that their simplicity was almost too profound, and a watchful eye was kept on their comings and goings. During the whole of this period the efficiency of the signal section was put to a very severe test from which they emerged with flying colours ; at this particular juncture they succeeded in maintaining communication with divisional headquarters ten miles away by helio and lamp by day and night respectively. On 7th March the battalion returned to Talat ed Dumm, and for the next two weeks preparations for the raid went on apace.

About midday on 20th March the battalion began to move down to the river valley. Our Brigade was to force the crossing, and the task allotted to the battalion was to get over at Makhadet-Hajlah, while 2/17th made a similar attempt at Ghoraniyeh. The river was unfordable and running fast, so the first crossing had to be effected by swimmers carrying a line by which a raft was to be pulled backwards and forwards. For this task Sec.-Lieut. G. E. Jones, of " A " Company, was selected as leader and a small party of volunteers was made up.

The battalion's objective for the night of 20th-21st was the Blue Dome Monastery, the occupants of which were very astonished to find nearly a whole battalion come squeezing into their precincts. " C " Company, under Capt. Radcliffe, took up an outpost position on the outskirts of the monastery garden. It was of crucial importance that no information as to our movements should reach the enemy, and so it had to be impressed on the monks that nobody must leave the monastery. What their language was we knew not and their knowledge of English was but slight. so the following dialogue took place, to the accompaniment of realistic pantomime, between the Battalion Intelligence Officer (Lieut. Woodroffe) and the Abbot, or whatever the head of the monastery was called :—

Woodroffe : " Monk leave monastery—soldier shoot."

Abbot : " That all right—not too much—not too much."

The meaning seems to have been understood, for nobody tried to leave, and there was no shooting, except that a man of " C " Company, on outpost, let his rifle off accidentally. The disturbance caused by this was as nothing compared with the outburst of righteous wrath from his company, for he was by no means a beginner. The signallers were able to send back messages by lamp to an advanced Corps Station, but no replies could be sent, of course, as they would have been visible to the enemy. Some New Zealand signallers brought up a cart to this point with a heavy cable and laid their line to within half a mile of the river, beyond which point it could not be taken on account of the noise the cart made ; the extension was laid by the battalion signallers by hand.

On the evening of the 21st the battalion moved down to the river. " A " and " C " Companies halted within a hundred yards of the bank, with " B " in support and " D " in reserve near Battalion Headquarters. Besides the two genuine attempts to cross, several feints were made at points up and down the stream from about midnight onwards. The attempt at Ghoraniyeh began at this hour, but the strength of the river was too great and the swimmers could not get across. By 1 a.m., when our own attempt was to be made, there was a considerable amount of enemy rifle and machine-gun fire going on, but luckily they had little idea of what was happening and the firing was quite at random. The position was critical, but Lieut. Jones with his gallant party, composed of Corporal Margrave, Lance-Corporal Henderson, Lance-Corporal Popham, Lance-Corporal Davis, Lance-Corporal Silver, Pte. Hardwick, Pte. Hoxton and Pte. Powell, succeeded in getting across, swimming with rifles strapped on their shoulders, and with the line they carried the first raft-load was pulled across at 1.20 a.m. Only eight men at a time could be carried on the raft, so it was a slow job getting the battalion over. Lieut. Mackay, of " A " Company, collected the first few raft-loads together and pushed a little distance into the thick undergrowth to protect as far as possible the crossing of the remainder.

This exploit of swimming the Jordan was one of great gallantry as well as picturesque and historic, and the names of the men taking part will long be remembered as adding to the Regiment's roll of honour. In recognition of their devotion and determination Lieut. Jones was awarded the Military Cross, Corporal Margrave the Military Medal and Lance-Corporal Popham the French Médaille Militaire. The signallers were able to report the success of the crossing within a few minutes of the event, and in consequence of the failure to get over at Ghoraniyeh, a complete change in the plan took place, and a considerable concentration was made at our crossing point at Makhadet-Hajlah.

The whole of " A " and " C " Companies were across before dawn without attracting the enemy's fire, but as it became light the position became clear to the Turk and the remainder of the crossing was

PONTOON BRIDGE—MAKHADET-HAJLAH, RIVER JORDAN.

REFUGEES FROM ES SALT CROSSING FOOTBRIDGE
AT GHORANIYEH, RIVER JORDAN.

made under heavy rifle and machine-gun fire. At first it was not easy to locate where it was coming from, but before long it was found that a hill about a thousand yards up stream was strongly held and thence enfilade fire was accurately directed ; in one raft-party of eight men, seven were hit. The 180th Machine Gun Company did fine work in providing covering fire, and by 7.15 a.m. the whole of the battalion was across.

The position on the far side of the river was rather confused. Lieut. Mackay was wounded, but Capt. Radcliffe took charge of both " A " and " C " Companies, and pushed out a line to the east and north to form a bridge-head. There was a belt of very thick undergrowth on the edge of the river bank, and beyond this it was almost impossible to advance in the face of rifle and machine-gun fire without artillery and other support.

It was soon evident that no further advance could be made without reinforcement. Capt. Chipperfield of 180th Machine Gun Company got some guns across and came into action on our right flank, giving exceedingly valuable covering fire. Meanwhile the Australian Engineers of the Desert Mounted Corps Bridging Train had by Herculean efforts completed a pontoon bridge a few hundred yards down stream from the spot where the battalion had crossed in rafts. By this means 2/18th Battalion crossed and came into position on our left, enabling us to side-step somewhat and reorganise.

With artillery support the advance began at 1.15 p.m. " B " and " D " were the attacking companies, with " A " and " C " in support. The task was to cross about three hundred yards of open ground and seize a line of sandhills. The movement was, however, foredoomed to failure. It was impossible to make any appreciable progress across the open in face of heavy rifle and machine-gun fire; nor could the troops get back to the cover, such as it was, in the wood, and they had to lie out until dark. The London Irish on our left had exactly the same experience. Our M.O. and his staff did what was possible for the wounded, but most of them could not be reached; some of the lesser cases tried to get back and were hit again on the way.

As night came on it was possible to estimate the losses. They were considerable, including Sergeants Hobbs and Pitt and Corporals Sims and Woodman, all killed. Advantage was also taken of the darkness to reconnoitre the position, but this was a very difficult task; one patrol consisting of Sec.-Lieut. E. Jones and four men were all killed and Lieut. Morris in command of another was wounded. One point which was established by reconnaissance was that there was a deep swamp on our front between us and the line of sandhills which were our objective.

The next attack was timed for midnight. The plan was roughly the same as that drawn up for the abortive attempt of the afternoon, except that " D " Company, who had suffered very severely, were replaced by " C " and the line of advance was modified to avoid the swamp. The 2/20th, however, had been substituted for the London Irish on our left. The first objectives were secured with little difficulty, the sandhills by the 2/19th and Chocolate Hill by 2/20th. As so often happened, however, the capture of one ridge only revealed another beyond which dominated it, and so the advance had to be extended a little farther to secure this position.

By this operation the bridgehead was established. At dawn the Australian mounted troops began to pass through and were able to clear away the enemy who had been holding up the crossing at El Ghoraniyeh. From the position we had now reached could be seen away to the north-east the heights of El Haud and Tel el Musta, covering Shunet Nimrin, which was the next objective for the infantry. The task, however, was allotted to 181st Brigade, as ours had had a very hard time during the last two days. Thus the battalion, temporarily relieved, was able to enjoy the experience of bathing in the River Jordan, to the enormous refreshment of all concerned. Next day, the 24th March, the battalion marched northwards to Ghoraniyeh over a deplorable sandy track.

On this day 179th and 181st Brigades captured their objectives and Shunet Nimrin was occupied. The 181st Brigade pushed up the road towards Es Salt in touch with Australian mounted troops. On 25th March the enemy evacuated Es Salt and a regiment of Australian Light Horse, followed by the 179th Brigade, occupied the town. The Australians made further progress towards Amman on 26th and a raiding party blew up part of the Hejaz railway seven miles south of the town. Next day two battalions of 181st Brigade marched towards Amman and the Australians and New Zealanders attempted to work round to the town from the north and south; several bridges and culverts on the railway were blown up. On

28th March the rest of 181st Brigade moved up towards Amman and a combined attack with the mounted troops was made on the place; but the position was very strong and held with great determination. Three battalions of 180th went up in support of 181st, but 2/19th remained in reserve. The enemy appeared to have been reinforced and on the 29th began to threaten our lines of communication. A night attack on Amman was launched at 2 a.m. on the 30th by all the troops available, but without achieving success. Meanwhile the situation in the neighbourhood of Es Salt was becoming threatening; a battalion of 179th Brigade was brought back and 2/19th were sent up to Howeij.

On the night of the 30th the withdrawal from Amman began. Heavy rains had caused the Jordan to rise nine feet, but in spite of this the bridges were maintained and the bulk of the force marched across on 31st March and 1st April. 2/19th remained at Howeij to cover the retirement of the units from Amman and Es Salt, and in the evening, acting as rearguard, withdrew to El Musta. It was a dreadful march over a track which had been almost crushed out of existence by the enormous traffic incidental to the advance and retirement of the raiding force. Much of it ran along the edge of almost sheer precipices, and there was no little danger of falling headlong where the road had been broken away more seriously even than the normal. The difficulties of the march were increased by the complication introduced by large numbers of natives, Bedouins and the like, who were fleeing westwards to escape the vengeance of the hated Turk.

The battalion remained at El Musta until noon on

the 2nd April, when a further retirement was made to the banks of the Jordan above El Ghoraniyeh, where they held the bridge-head. The position was practically that held by the enemy when the crossing was first attempted, but facing, of course, the other way, east instead of west. Next morning Turkish cavalry were spotted coming down the road and soon a brisk outpost action was in progress; we had good artillery support from the west side of the Jordan valley and the enemy did not press home the attack. In the afternoon the battalion was relieved by the Australian Light Horse, who continued to hold the bridge-head until the conclusion of hostilities six months later, except for the period of the second Amman raid. The battalion marched back across the pontoon bridge and up the long, weary climb into the Judæan Hills, where eventually they bivouacked.

So ended the first raid across Jordan. The battalion had been the first unit to cross and was the last of the Division to return. The primary object of the expedition—to interrupt the communications along the Hejaz Railway—had been achieved, and, incidentally, the impression had been given to the enemy that our ultimate advance was to be made on the east side of the Jordan, with the result that they had to keep their forces dispersed over a wide area from the Mediterranean eastwards. The losses of the battalion had been heavy, not only in action, but by sickness; for the climatic conditions were exceptionally trying, varying as they did from the humid heat in the malarial valley 1,200 feet below sea-level to the still wintry conditions in the hills towards Es Salt and Amman.

CHAPTER XV.
SECOND JORDAN RAID.

During the first two weeks of April the battalion remained in the plain of Jericho in support of the Imperial Camel Corps and Australian mounted troops, who were holding the line of the Jordan and the bridge-head at Ghoraniyeh. The climatic conditions were very trying, and in spite of the most rigorous precautions there was a good deal of sickness, malaria for the most part. The enemy had been considerably reinforced east of the Jordan and had made several unsuccessful attempts to recapture the bridge-head. On 14th April the battalion moved up to the comparatively cool and pleasant area at Talat ed Dumm, but on the 18th they were back again in the valley making a demonstration to distract the attention of the enemy. On the 21st a move was made right back to the Mount of Olives, overlooking Jerusalem, and rumours were current that the next move would be to the coast. But this was too good to be true, for once more the whole Division was destined to return to the Jordan valley, with its intense heat and trying conditions, for another spell of hard fighting.

The object of this new move was in part to confirm the enemy's impression that the Commander-in-Chief intended to make his final advance on the eastern side of the river, in part to help the Hedjaz army by cutting the railway line near Amman and thereby interrupting the communications of the

ES SALT—A TYPICAL HILL VILLAGE IN PALESTINE.

TURKS MAKING ROAD BETWEEN JERUSALEM AND BETHLEHEM.

enemy forces acting against them, and in part to strengthen the wavering enthusiasm of some of the Arab tribesmen who inhabited the area.

Whatever may have been at the back of the Commander-in-Chief's mind, by the night of 28th April the battalion was once more among the foothills of the bridge-head at Ghoraniyeh. The 179th and 180th Brigades were to attack the much strengthened positions at El Haud and Shunet Nimrin, while the Desert Mounted Corps made a detour northwards to Es Salt.

The battalion moved off at 10.30 p.m. on the 29th, through the belt of wire which had been constructed to protect the bridge-head, and deployed to the right of the main road to Es Salt, the 179th Brigade being to the left of it. 2/20th Battalion were immediately to the left of the road with Tel-el-Bilibel as their objective : to the 2/19th on their right was allotted Derbasil as objective and a company of 2/17th acted as right flank guard. " A " and " C " Companies were in front, " B " in support, and " D " in battalion reserve. " A " Company was now commanded by Capt. Egerton, an officer attached from the Black Watch, and " C " Company by Capt. Radcliffe. There was not much moon and it was therefore difficult to keep direction and proper intervals and distances between platoons. Much of the advance was through fields of growing corn, which was waist-high or higher. In the faint light the line of the hills ahead was just visible and, although steady progress was made, for a long time they seemed to come no nearer. In the early stages there was no opposition from the enemy and the only sound was the chirping of myriads of crickets. The whole affair seemed unreal until soon after midnight there was an outburst of rifle and machine-gun fire away to the left, which showed that 179th Brigade was in touch with the enemy.

Our first objective was reached without opposition, at 2.15 a.m. and at 2.45 the " caves " were occupied. But no further progress could be made, for the enemy were holding a *sangar* line just beyond and " A " and " C " Companies were driven back to the caves with heavy loss. " A " Company suffered very severely : Lieut. Gambell and Lieut. Hardy were killed and Capt. Egerton was so severely wounded that he died later. Much reduced in numbers the two companies sheltered in the caves and Capt. Radcliffe organised a defence. As day dawned further attempts were made to get forward, but before long it became evident that it was equally impossible to go forward or back. There were many wounded collected in the caves and the stretcher bearers were ably assisted in the work of tending them by Padre Motley, who had gone forward with " C " Company. Lieut. Woodroffe, Battalion Intelligence Officer, was also with Capt. Radcliffe.

It appeared that 2/20th on our left were in similar plight. The right flank company of 2/17th was also held up, and " B " Company of 2/19th were unable to make any progress in an attempt to reinforce them. So depleted were " A " and " C " Companies in numbers that they could hardly have withstood a determined enemy counter-attack. Attempts were made to send up reinforcements to the battalion from the 2/17th, but very few were able to get across the exposed and open ground. The signallers' wires were soon cut by shell fire, but very gallant efforts were made to restore communications. Lance-Corporal Speed, of the signal section, came alone along the line from battalion H.Q. under heavy fire, repairing breaks, and seemed to have a charmed life ; eventually he was hit, however, but he managed to reach the caves. Corporal H. Beamish, who had been a member of the section from its formation, set out from battalion H.Q. with two linesmen on the same task ; finding that the fire was very heavy he sent his two companions back and went on alone, but was never seen again.

The position of the advanced companies was precarious in the extreme when the sentries reported about noon that the enemy appeared to be forming up for a counter-attack. Capt. Radcliffe made what preparations were possible to meet the emergency, and considerable loss was inflicted on the enemy with rifle grenades and bombs, so close were they. Our artillery were firing on the enemy positions at long range, but some of their shells fell short and inflicted casualties upon the devoted force in the caves. Fortunately, about this time a fresh attempt to advance on Bilibel caused a diversion on the left, and the enemy counter-attack was not pressed home.

As it turned out, the crisis had now passed, but the position was one of extreme anxiety for the remaining six or seven hours of daylight. As dusk fell it became possible to get the wounded away on improvised stretchers, and later the surviving remnant were able to withdraw after one of the most trying days the battalion had experienced during the whole war. It is not too much to say that it was the resolution and splendid leadership displayed by

Capt. Radcliffe which saved the situation from complete disaster. 2/17th Battalion relieved us in the front line and "D" Company 2/19th were attached in close support to them. They made a further attempt on the enemy position, but with no greater success than had attended ours. Towards midnight on the 1st-2nd May a fresh attack was organised, and 16th Platoon of our "D" Company was attached to "C" Company of 2/17th, who had suffered heavy casualties. The attack seemed to be going well when a party, including Sergt. Crane and several of our 16th Platoon, walked into an enemy post in mistake for one of our own. After a gallant resistance and suffering heavy losses they were forced to surrender. On this day Pte. Scammell, who had been awarded the D.C.M. for gallantry at Nebi Samwil, was killed, and Sergt. Fry, another D.C.M., was killed on the first day of the advance.

On the evening of 2nd May the battalion again relieved 2/17th and held an outpost line until the night of the 4th, when the whole division was withdrawn across the Jordan. In the meantime the Australian Mounted Division had made their dash, but they had encountered very serious resistance and had withdrawn with some difficulty from their isolated positions.

After the earlier raid across the Jordan the enemy on this part of the front had been considerably reinforced and his positions much strengthened. This factor, although it worked so much to our disadvantage when the second raid came to be made, constituted, nevertheless, a satisfactory development of General Allenby's main scheme, for it implied that the Turks had scattered their available forces over a wider front.

The total casualties of the battalion during the second raid amounted to 136, of whom 33 were reported missing at the time, but mostly accounted for later.

———

CHAPTER XVI.

Reorganisation and Final Victory.

On the 6th May the battalion was back on the Mount of Olives, and on the 7th it proceeded to a reserve camp at Ramallah on the Nablus Road. For a few days a well-earned and badly needed spell of rest ensued, enlivened by sports, a horse show, concerts and the like. In spite of the gruelling they had been through the men quickly responded to this treatment and were soon in fine form again.

It must be borne in mind that the period we have now reached was one of extreme crisis on the Western Front. Beginning on the 21st March the enemy, strongly reinforced from the Russian Front, had made a desperate attack on the French and our Fifth Army, and had almost succeeded in breaking through between the French and ourselves and reaching Amiens. It had become a matter of the most urgent importance to send every possible fighting man to France pending the expected arrival of the vast American armies. It was therefore decided to draw heavily upon the Egyptian Expeditionary Force, which was largely composed of seasoned troops. Two whole infantry divisions, the 52nd (Lowland Scottish) and 74th (Dismounted Yeomanry), were transported bodily; and seven to nine battalions from each of the other five divisions, leaving only three battalions to each. The depleted divisions were made up to strength with newly raised Indian formations. In addition a considerable number of

A BIVOUAC, JUDEAN HILLS.

TURKISH DESERTERS AT MEZRAH ESH SHERKIYEH.

batteries of artillery were sent to France. In the 60th Division only 2/13th, 2/19th and 2/22nd battalions, one in each Brigade, remained. 2/18th and 2/21st were disbanded, and the others—including our old comrades in the 180th Brigade, the 2/17th and 2/20th—went to France. The Indian battalions allotted to our Brigade were the 2nd Guides Infantry, the 2/30th Punjabis and the 1/50th Kumaon Rifles.

It was naturally with real regret that we parted from our friends, and equally natural that we should feel anxiety as to how the Division would shake down under the new conditions. It was one point to the good that General Shea, the divisional commander, was an Indian Army officer of great experience.

The Indian battalions were newly raised and had a very small proportion of Indian Army officers who knew the language and understood the idiosyncrasies of their men. The supply problem became one of even greater difficulty than before because of the varied requirements of the Indian troops, largely the result of their religious beliefs. Altogether there seemed little likelihood of welding the new force into an efficient fighting machine for many months ahead, and who could say what might happen in the meantime?

During the period of transition the battalion was temporarily attached to 53rd Division and took over a section of the line at Sheikh Selim on the right of the Nablus Road. The section included a position known as Highgate Ridge, a name familiar and welcome to London troops. The summer months passed very quietly, but it soon became apparent that an offensive on a very large scale was in preparation, much sooner than had been thought possible. Even when the battalion was in the line training for the offensive was not overlooked and units in reserve were put through an intensive course.

No inkling of the plan of campaign leaked out for a long time. A force was kept in the Jordan valley, the bridge-head at Ghoraniyeh still being held, and the enemy continued to cling to the idea that the great effort would be made there. Actually, however, the scheme was to make a vast concentration of troops on the coast sector at the opposite end of the line.

General Allenby's plan may be thus outlined. The main attack was to be made on the extreme left by XXI Corps, commanded by General Bulfin; the 54th Division being on the right of the Corps front, then the 3rd Indian, the 75th, and the 7th Indian, with the 60th on the left reaching the sea. Pivoting on the right the whole Corps, about 30,000 rifles, was to wheel north and east to Tul Keram, Sebustiye and Nablus; 5th Australian Light Horse Brigade was attached to the Corps for the operation. As soon as the infantry had forced their way through the enemy line on the coast sector, General Chauvel's Desert Mounted Corps, consisting of 4th and 5th Cavalry Divisions (largely Indian) and the Australian Mounted Division, were to pour through the gap and make a dash for El Afule, an important railway junction which it was hoped to reach on the second day. This objective was forty miles from the original British front line and only six or seven miles short of Nazareth, where the enemy Headquarters were situated; and an effort was to be made to take them by surprise and, if possible, to capture Liman von Sanders, the German Commander-in-Chief, and his staff. General Chetwode's XXth Corps, consisting of 53rd and 10th Divisions, was to advance meanwhile on either side of the Nablus Road. The gap between these two advancing Corps, and also the Jordan valley, were to be held lightly by Watson's and Chaytor's Forces, with instructions to conform as far as possible to the main advance.

It was hoped that by this boldly conceived scheme the XXIst Corps would cut off the communications and line of retreat of the main Turkish armies holding the line, while the cavalry in conjunction with the Air Force would spread havoc in the back areas, prevent any possibility of rushing up reserves for a counter-attack, and completely paralyse the whole enemy " supply " service.

The most elaborate arrangements were, of course, necessary. The great concentration of troops near the coast was carried out without the enemy being aware of it, as was shown later by captured situation maps which marked divisions at places which in some cases they had left a week or more before. To achieve this secrecy many devices were adopted. All movement westward was made by night, and such as was necessary eastward by day. Evacuated camps and bivouacs were left standing. During the daytime troops were encamped either under cover in orange groves, etc., or in camps which had long existed. All this of course was to mislead enemy aircraft, but the supremacy established by our own airmen gave hostile planes little chance of reconnoitring our side of the line.

It was recognised that at the best it would be impossible to keep up supplies for the Mounted Corps, and they were warned that for a day or two they might have to live on the country, although they were to take with them about four days' rations, and machinery for developing water supply. For the water question was still a difficult one, though not so insuperable in the Galilean Hills as it had been in the Beersheba operations of the previous autumn. The bulk of the artillery too was concentrated on XXIst Corps' front to secure that the infantry should be able to break through with the least possible delay. Communications were likely to be a cause of anxiety; but it was hoped that, as a result of the suddenness of the advance, it would be possible to make use of enemy wires, while, owing to the clear atmosphere and good light, visual signalling was found very useful.

Our aerial reconnaissance had disclosed that on the coast sector the enemy had three organised lines of defence, weaker in order from front to rear. The main anxiety, however, was not whether the defences would prove too strong, but whether or not the enemy had evacuated them. It was almost too much to hope that such a mighty concentration had been effected without the enemy discovering it, and that he would wait to be entrapped " according to plan." In the event the whole scheme worked almost without hitch, and the magnitude of the success exceeded all expectations.

Zero hour was fixed for 4.30 a.m. on 19th September. There was no preliminary bombardment, and the infantry advanced at the moment the guns opened fire. Immense was the relief of all concerned to see that thousands of signal rockets at once soared into the air, showing that the enemy were still holding the line in strength. The moon was still up when the attack began, so all could get an idea of their direction, but after it went down there was half-an-hour of complete darkness before the first streak of dawn, and good use was made of this time to advance rapidly before the enemy could see clearly what was happening.

The task allotted to 60th Division was a most exacting one and made great demands upon both fighting ability and powers of endurance. During the last week in August the Division had been relieved in the hills on either side of the Nablus Road, and for about a fortnight it had undergone a course of intensive training for the great effort which was to be required of it—its rôle being to form the outside edge of the right-wheeling movement of XXIst Corps and to open the way for the cavalry. Between 15th and 18th September the Division had moved up into position by a series of night marches, and at Zero hour on the 19th it was disposed in depth on its front. 180th Brigade was leading, 181st in support, and 179th in divisional reserve. It must be remembered that the constitution of the Division now was very different from what it had been during its previous operations, Indian units, mostly newly raised, having taken the place of most of the veteran London battalions by whose side we were accustomed to go into action. Brigadier-General Watson, however, remained in command of 180th Brigade. The 2/19th was commanded, as was fitting in this climax to its varied experiences, by Major C. S. Williamson, M.C., an officer who had been with the battalion continuously since its formation in Camden Town four years before, and who had shared in all its hardships and successes.

When the opening of the bombardment gave the signal for the advance the leading battalions dashed forward, the Kumaon Rifles on the right and the Guides on the left, both units going into action for the first time; another Indian battalion, 2/97th of 181st Brigade, was attached for the purpose of capturing a strong redoubt on the right. The first objectives were carried within a few minutes and many prisoners and several machine guns captured. The attack on the redoubt by 2/97th was to have been covered by a smoke screen dropped from an aeroplane, but the redoubt was captured before the aeroplane arrived. All the objectives were taken by 5.40; and 2/19th went through, forced the passage of the Nahr-el-Falik with some loss, and established the bridge-head on the far side at 7.20. This done, the 5th Cavalry Division began to pass through within a few minutes. In less than three hours the Brigade had advanced, in some cases, 6,000 yards, and had captured three lines of enemy trenches, about 600 prisoners and many machine guns. The casualties, however, were rather heavy, being 414 distributed over the five battalions, including 2/97th attached. The Nahr-el-Falik was running so low that there was no need to build a bridge.

181st Brigade took up the advance at 8.30, and 5th Light Horse Brigade began its dash for Tul Keram, or rather the road leading east from it to Nablus. Passing round the west and north of the town they cut in on the road and captured 2,000 prisoners with 15 guns.

Meanwhile, 181st Brigade reached Tul Keram by 5 p.m., having taken 800 prisoners and a dozen guns. The Air Force contributed greatly to the victory, for they raided far over the enemy's lines and wrought fearful havoc with bombs and machine-gun fire on the roads, along which by now endless streams of transport and fugitives were pressing.

By nightfall the division had accomplished all its tasks, and was formed up on a line running roughly north and south with its left at Tul Keram. The day had been one calling forth the greatest powers of endurance, for after seizing their objectives in the early morning the troops had to push on through the heat of the day over heavy country; in some cases upwards of 16 miles had been covered in these conditions during the day, and that by troops in full battle order.

The other divisions of the Corps, and the XXth Corps advancing northwards on Nablus, met with more serious opposition. But the successes of 60th Division and especially of the Mounted Corps made further resistance by the enemy fruitless, and by 22nd September the whole of the line Tul Keram-Nablus was in our hands and the cavalry were much farther north, as far as Nazareth. The success of the XXIst Corps had been stupendous. Practically the whole of the Turkish 8th Army had ceased to exist; 12,000 prisoners were taken and 149 guns, and vast quantities of ammunition and transport were either captured or destroyed.

CHAPTER XVII.
THE LAST OF THE 2/19TH.

In the remainder of the campaign the battalion took no further active part. Nor, indeed, did any of the infantry, for movement was so rapid and continuous that only mounted troops were of any use. The wonderful feats of endurance of the cavalry and their overwhelming successes, in co-operation of course with the raids of the Air Force, are part of the general history of the War. Let it suffice here to say that Nazareth was reached on 22nd September, Haifa on 24th and Damascus on 30th. At this stage of the advance about 150 miles had been covered in twelve days and most of the Turkish Army overwhelmed and cut off on the way. Beirut was occupied on 8th October, and Aleppo on 26th, this being upwards of another 200 miles.

While these dashing exploits were being achieved by the cavalry the 2/19th, with the rest of 60th Division, was engaged in the more prosaic duty of clearing up the wreckage of the Turkish Army on the lines of communication. 75,000 prisoners had to be shepherded down the line, large numbers of them sick or wounded and all the rest in a dreadful state of exhaustion and privation. Vast quantities of stores of all kinds had to be collected and disposed of; the sites of some of the air raids on retreating columns of guns and transport were appalling scenes of devastation. On 23rd September the battalion was at Kalkilieh and on 24th moved to Fejja; on 30th we were at Mulebbis, only a few miles from Jaffa, and subsequent camping grounds in the neighbourhood were at Sarona and Yasur. During all this time our hands had been kept very full with salvage work, escorting prisoners, and so on.

On 9th November the battalion entrained for Kantara and arrived there on the following afternoon. Meanwhile an Armistice had been concluded with the Turks, coming into force on 31st October. The general Armistice with Germany followed, of course, on 11th November, the day after the 2/19th reached Kantara. On 16th a move was made to Sidi Bishr near Alexandria.

From this point onwards the history of the battalion becomes one of gradual dissolution. Christmas was kept at Alexandria with suitable celebrations, including a horse race for officers, but one's mind would hark back to the previous Christmas in Jerusalem and the one before that at Spancova Farm on the hills of Macedonia, and to all that had happened in the meanwhile.

The process of demobilisation soon began; some lucky ones got away quite soon. Trouble began to brew among the Egyptians and in March some demonstration of force became necessary to restore order in Alexandria. On 16th the battalion left Sidi Bishr for Port Said, where we embarked with 22nd London for Beirut *en route* for Homs.

On 24th March the battalion was amalgamated with the 2nd Battalion of the Leicestershire Regt., but it preserved its identity as H.Q. of the Leicesters left for home. On 3rd April the composite battalion moved on to Aleppo. The duty of the military garrison was to preserve law and order, but it was not a very arduous one, and sport bulked large in the activities. This unexciting existence continued for six months.

In October large drafts of men from a battalion of the Suffolk Regt. were posted to the battalion ; the process of absorption was not very easy, and not welcome to either party, but eventually we settled down again.

In December the battalion was back again at Kantara and on the 23rd provided a guard of honour of 100 men, under Capt. Ashdown, for Lord Allenby. It was fitting that an officer who had played so distinguished a part in nearly all the greater achievements of the 2/19th should have taken part also in what was to be one of the last public appearances of the battalion.

Yet another Christmas, the sixth, was celebrated, but the end was at hand. Officers and men were fast fading away, and about the middle of February, 1920, the 2/19th London Regt., after an existence of about five and a half years, was finally wound up.

* * * * * * *

The active life of the battalion lasted barely four years, the last eighteen months being something of an anti-climax. It does not sound a long period, but into that comparatively short space was crowded a wealth of experience which sufficed to build up a corporate spirit equal to that of corps whose histories go back hundreds of years.

In one respect the battalion enjoyed an immense advantage over many whose active service experience was confined to the Western Front. At no time was it subjected to the devastating casualties, which made it necessary for units to be practically reconstituted perhaps twice or three times within a few months. The average length of service of officers and men with the 2/19th was much longer than in battalions in France, and consequently all ranks got to know one another better, and moreover had the experience necessary to secure the best possible conditions of life, and the best chances of success in action. Certain it is that there was a spirit in 2/19th which carried the battalion through many trials and some glorious episodes and to this day holds most of its members of all ranks together in a comradeship which they are ever proud to own.

The battalion was very fortunate in its commanding officers. To Col. Christie fell the lot of raising the 2/19th and of welding a mob of enthusiastic but almost entirely inexperienced civilians into a military organisation. This in depressing conditions he succeeded in doing, not only in the strictly military sense by instilling discipline and sound principles of training, but even more by the exercise of those qualities of common sense, tact and good humour which characterised him as a man. Col. Sword took over the command for the last intensive period of training on Salisbury Plain before going overseas. A much younger man, and a regular soldier with experience on the Western Front, he came to us with orders to " ginger us up," and he carried them out to the letter. He did not seek popularity or expect it, but as soon as the battalion reached the front line it realised the value of his training and his sterling qualities as a soldier. His period of command covered our spell in France, where his enthusiasm and personal courage were an inspiration to every officer and man, the dreary months in Macedonia, where he succeeded in preserving the *moral* of the men in conditions in which its decay was only too common, and the first and hardest part of the Palestine Campaign until after the fall of Jerusalem, in which 2/19th established a reputation second to none as a fighting unit.

During the two Jordan raids the battalion was commanded by Major Craddock of 2/20th, who was generous in his tribute to the fine qualities of the men under him.

When the E.E.F. was reorganised in the summer of 1918, following the dispatch of many British units to France, the command of 2/19th fell to Col. Norton, who had previously commanded 2/18th in the same brigade and was therefore no stranger; and he held the position until the dissolution of the battalion early in 1920, except during very short spells. One of these happened to fall in September, 1918, when Major Williamson, one of the original officers of the battalion, commanded for the final advance.

All of these officers contributed their part to the battalion's history, and they have all acknowledged the debt which they, and the battalion as a whole, owe to R.S.M. Manning, who held his most important post from the formation of the unit until after the Armistice. From the first he set a very high standard for the non-commissioned officers to aim at : he maintained it to the end, and without any doubt very much of the success achieved by 2/19th was due to the fine quality of the men he trained.

It has been said that an army advances on its stomach, which is a picturesque way of emphasising the importance of the Quartermaster's Dept. Capt. Edgar Bleeze held that most responsible position from before our leaving England until after the Armistice, and right well did he serve the battalion. Not only did we get whatever we were entitled to, but thanks to the foresight and untiring energy of our Quartermaster we often had unexpected little comforts which less fortunate units had to do without. And the Quartermaster himself is not the only man in his Department who can make or mar the happiness of the troops. Until the move was made to Salonika Bleeze had as his right-hand man R.Q.M.S. de Beaurepaire, and afterwards R.Q.M.S. Earl, both of whom brought their long service with the 19th to an end by filling this most responsible position on active service.

Another familiar figure in the "Q" Dept. was Sergt. Windust, a veteran of the South African War, who from start to finish of the life of 2/19th was connected with the drawing and issue of rations.

Second only to the commissariat in importance— and perhaps it is a dead heat—is the department of "Communications." The "Signals" section, "L.O.S." as it was called in code (L.O. standing for London and S being the 19th letter of the alphabet), from the earliest days had a high reputation for efficiency and for *esprit de corps*. The good work begun by Capt. V. A. Elgood in building up the section was carried on by Capt. Ashdown, and each had the untiring and loyal assistance of Sergt. W. Langlois, whose methods of securing discipline among his men, though perhaps unorthodox, were highly successful.

The Transport section was another which contributed very materially to the welfare of the battalion. The foundations of its efficiency were laid by Lieut. Harden, and the fruits of his good work were gathered in many a dreary spot where it would hardly have been thought possible for even a " limber G.S.," though drawn by those irrepressible mules, to have penetrated.

Much of course must be credited to Commanding Officers, and much to specialist sections, but it is to the ordinary man in the ranks of the company that the final tribute of praise must be paid for the wonderful deeds performed by the battalion. What splendid fellows they were ! They were Londoners for the most part, drawn from offices, factories, shops and every conceivable occupation ; but the big draft of men transferred from the R.A.M.C. just before we went to France contained men from all parts of the country, especially Wales and the North, and these added diverse elements. But the spirit of the battalion, by that time well established, proved equal to absorbing them all into the body corporate and they proved a most useful addition. It did not seem to matter what was the task allotted, the men were always equal to it. Trudging along filthy communication trenches, carrying enormous loads, making a dashing raid on the enemy's line, or consolidating a mine crater, it was all the same to them. In Macedonia they struggled through incredible mud or endured the icy blasts of a Vardar blizzard with equal good temper. The dust and thirst of Beersheba and Sheria they took for granted, as they did the fierce bombardment on the exposed ridge at Nebi Samwil, and the arduous climb to Deir Yesin under intense machine-gun fire. The stifling heat of the Jordan Valley and the horrible day in the caves of Shunet Nimrin did not shake them.

Whatever task came their way they performed with the same unaffected nonchalance; it never seemed to occur to them that it was at all extraordinary. They generally had some little joke to work off on their pals, or some quite insignificant grievance against them.

That such feats of courage and endurance could be performed by unmilitarised citizens, many of them as lacking in muscular strength as they were in the arts of war, would have seemed incredible a few years earlier to most people, and especially incredible to the men themselves. It was, perhaps, in under-estimating the capabilities of such soldiers as these that the German War Lords made one of their greatest mistakes, a mistake which contributed its full share to the winning and losing of the War. At all events, it is peculiarly fitting and quite inevitable that a History of the 2/19th London Regiment should close with a tribute to the qualities of the men who served in its ranks.

APPENDIX I.

CASUALTY LISTS.

K. in A. = Killed in Action.
D. of W. = Died of Wounds.
D. = Died.
W. = Wounded.
K. = Killed.

In the casualty lists for France only those wounded and evacuated to the United Kingdom are given.

FRANCE (June—December, 1916).

Name.	Regtl. No.	Rank.	Date.	Nature of Casualty.	Action.
Clayton, F.	3430	Sgt.	10.7.16	K. (accident)	France.
Gray, H. H.	6244	Pte.	13.7.16	D. of W.	,,
Bennett, J.	6183	Pte.	13.7.16	W.	,,
Seymour, C.	3954	Pte.	20.7.16	W.	,,
Brigden, W. H.	5002	Pte.	26.7.16	K. in A.	,,
Proctor, F. J.	6427	L./Sgt.	27.7.16	D. of W.	,,
Haugh, D.	6262	Pte.	28.7.16	K. in A.	,,
Lester, W. G.	3354	Pte.	30.7.16	D. of W.	,,
Rosemburg, J.	5351	Pte.	9.8.16	W.	,,
Tyndall, J.		2/Lieut.	11.8.16	W.	,,
Edgar, H.	4738	Pte.	11.8.16	K. in A.	,,
Willis, H. A.	2657	Dmr.	11.8.16	K. in A.	,,
Gospel, C. W.	6249	Pte.	11.8.16	K. in A.	,,
Lee, T. W.	3308	Pte.	12.8.16	D. of W.	,,
Stables, H. R.	6352	Pte.	12.8.16	W.	,,
Bibbings, E. G. C.	6177	Pte.	12.8.16	K. in A.	,,
Pethen, G. W.	6318	Pte.	13.8.16	D. of W.	,,
Briffett, H. J.	6179	Pte.	13.8.16	D. of W.	,,
Russell, C.	6638	Pte.	14.8.16	W.	,,
Murray, C.	6460	Pte.	15.8.16	W.	,,
Bamber, T.	4628	Pte.	15.8.16	W.	,,
Harvey, L.	1010	Pte.	16.8.16	K. in A.	,,
Delahaye, C.	6228	Pte.	16.8.16	K. in A.	,,
Kelly, H. E.	4891	Pte.	16.8.16	K. in A.	,,
Merriman, R. E.	2462	Pte.	17.8.16	K. in A.	,,
Lambert, S.	2300	Pte.	18.8.16	D. of W.	,,
Zambra, A.	6499	Pte.	19.8.16	W.	,,
Bevan, H.	5103	L./Cpl.	20.8.16	W.	,,
Ruth, R.	6330	Pte.	20.8.16	W.	,,
Smith	5559	Rfn. (9th Lon. attached.)	21.8.16	W.	,,
Barrell, J. W.	6893	L./Cpl.	21.8.16	W.	,,
Naylor, M.	6308	Pte.	21.8.16	W.	,,
Murphy, J.	6304	Pte.	24.8.16	W.	,,
Rickard, A. C.	6334	Pte.	24.8.16	W.	,,
Bumby, F.	2136	Cpl.	25.8.16	K. in A.	,,
Archer, F. A.	4373	Cpl.	26.8.16	W.	,,
Gilmour, J.	6246	Pte.	26.8.16	W.	,,
Bromhead	6169	Sgt.	28.8.16	W.	,,
Large, D.	6458	Pte.	2.9.16	W.	,,
Waits, A.	6405	Pte.	2.9.16	W.	,,
Chapple, R. R. M.	3395	Sgt.	4.9.16	W.	,,
Williams, W. A.		2/Lieut.	5.9.16	W.	,,
Hicks, W. H.	4598	Pte.	5.9.16	W.	,,

Name.	Regtl. No.	Rank.	Date.	Nature of Casualty.	Action.
Sumpton, A. W.	5382	Pte.	6.9.16	K. in A.	France.
Church, W. G.	6430	Pte.	6.9.16	K. in A.	,,
Bagshaw, J.	6198	Pte.	6.9.16	K. in A.	,,
Mager, A. H.	6302	Pte.	8.9.16	W.	,,
Joynson, R.	6280	Pte.	8.9.16	K. in A.	,,
Berks, A. W.	4478	Pte.	9.9.16	K. in A.	,,
Wharfe, E.	3497	Pte.	10.9.16	W.	,,
Owen, A. K.	6312	L./Cpl.	16.9.16	W.	,,
Forster, H.	5631	Pte.	18.9.16	W.	,,
Stockwell, C. J.	4841	Pte.	20.9.16	K. in A.	,,
White, G. E.	6383	Pte.	20.9.16	D. of W.	,,
Schonfield, E.		Lieut.	20.9.16	K. in A.	,,
Montague, F. H.	4760	Rfn. (1/9 Lon. attached.)	20.9.16	W.	,,
Winterton, F.	1714	Pte.	25.9.16	W.	,,
Worsfold, A. H.	3746	Pte.	25.9.16	W.	,,
Owen, T. J.	5004	Pte.	28.9.16	D. of W.	,,
Stead, C.	6368	Pte.	5.10.16	W.	,,
Ordway, E. A.	2928	Sgt.	6.10.16	W.	,,
Smith, E. C.	6504	Pte.	8.10.16	W.	,,
Richards, G.	6314	Pte.	8.10.16	W.	,,
Morris, J.	6303	Pte.	9.10.16	W.	,,
Vaile, P. A.		2/Lieut.	14.10.16	K. (accident)	,,
Beynon, A.	6193	Pte.	15.10.16	K. in A.	,,
Stevenson, E.	6353	L./Cpl.	15.10.16	K. in A.	,,
Wells, D.	6396	Pte.	16.10.16	K. in A.	,,
Tointon, H. W.	3191	Sgt.	26.10.16	W.	,,
Dunn, J. H.	6410	Pte.	28.10.16	W.	,,

MACEDONIA (December, 1916—June, 1917).

Name.	Regtl. No.	Rank.	Date.	Nature of Casualty.	Action.
Jeans, C. F.	6273	Pte.	21.12.16	Died (appendicitis)	Macedonia.
Colyer, W. E. F.	614066	Pte.	27.2.17	W.	,,
Knight, W.	533993	Pte.	27.2.17	W.	,,
Hearnshaw, J.	611402	Dmr.	18.3.17	W.	,,
Isaacs, F.	611892	Pte.	18.3.17	W.	,,
Leonard, W.	611582	Pte.	18.3.17	W.	,,
Merriman, A. H.	611926	Pte.	18.3.17	W.	,,
Cade, P. G.	612482	Pte.	18.3.17	W.	,,
Wayland, W.	612721	Pte.	18.3.17	W.	,,

Name	Regtl. No.	Rank	Date	Nature of Casualty	Action
Charing, J.	4607	Pte.	18.3.17	W.	Macedonia.
Jacobs, J.	4771	Pte.	18.3.17	W.	,,
Gould, G. J.	533790	Pte.	22.3.17	W.	,,
Perfect, R. S.	613931	Pte.	5.4.17	D. of W.	,,
Batchelor, F. G.	613910	Pte.	5.4.17	D. of W.	,,
Simmons, A.	613935	Pte.	5.4.17	D. of W.	,,
Hart, H. T.	613877	Pte.	5.4.17	D. of W.	,,
Church, E. H.	611291	Pte.	5.4.17	K. in A.	,,
Drayton, A. W.	613918	Pte.	5.4.17	W.	,,
Mansfield, G. W.	613926	Pte.	5.4.17	W.	,,
Strain, F.	613938	Pte.	5.4.17	W.	,,
Palmer, A. W.	613928	Pte.	5.4.17	W.	,,
Smith, E. J.	613056	Pte.	5.4.17	W.	,,
Treays, E. A.	614116	Pte.	7.4.17	W.	,,
Dopson, E. J.	612685	Pte.	4.5.17	W.	,,
Dopson, E. J.	612685	Pte.	18.5.17	D. of W.	,,

PALESTINE (June, 1917—December, 1918).

Name	Regtl. No.	Rank	Date	Nature of Casualty	Action
Goodfellow, W. E.	612743	Pte.	26.6.17	D.	Palestine.
Webb, A.	610976	L./Sgt.	8.7.17	W. (accident)	,,
Taylor, W. G.	614326	Pte.	20.10.17	W. (accident)	,,
Cooper, J.	611192	Pte.	31.10.17	K. in A.	Beersheba.
Wright, A. J.	610826	Pte.	3.11.17	D.	,,
McDougall, A.	612553	Pte.	3.11.17	W.	,,
Darvell, S. D.	612736	Pte.	3.11.17	W.	,,
Sealey, A. H.	611722	Pte.	3.11.17	W.	,,
Vincent, W. J.		2/Lieut.	6.11.17	W.	Kauwaukah.
Green, W. R.	612693	Pte.	6.11.17	K. in A.	,,
Grandjean, R. P.	611329	Pte.	6.11.17	W.	,,
Bradley, H. T.	612673	Pte.	6.11.17	W.	,,
Bright, W.	610927	Cpl.	6.11.17	W.	,,
Brown, W.	613913	Pte.	6.11.17	W.	,,
Deighton, F.	613715	Pte.	6.11.17	W.	,,
Gamage, J. W.	613874	Pte.	6.11.17	W.	,,
Hinds, C. H.	611041	Pte.	6.11.17	W.	,,
Martin, W. R.	613885	Pte.	6.11.17	W.	,,
Richardson, A.	611779	Pte.	6.11.17	W.	,,
Robinson, C. J.	612809	Pte.	6.11.17	W.	,,
Scapons, R. J.	610370	Dmr.	6.11.17	W.	,,
Snelling, C.	613956	Pte.	6.11.17	W.	,,
Cornwell, H. J.	614417	Pte.	6.11.17	W.	,,

Name.	Regtl. No.	Rank.	Date.	Nature of Casualty.	Action.
GRAY, A. J.		Major	7.11.17	K. in A.	Sheria.
ASHTON, R. M. (D.C.M.)		2/Lieut.	7.11.17	K. in A.	,,
CLAY, C.	614462	Pte.	7.11.17	D. of W.	,,
BOOTHER, A. R.	614414	Pte.	7.11.17	D. of W.	,,
BOOTHBY, H. J.	610883	Pte.	7.11.17	K. in A.	,,
DESBOIS, R. C.	613979	Pte.	7.11.17	K. in A.	,,
FISHER, F. A.	610348	Pte.	7.11.17	K. in A.	,,
FLYNN, G.	610982	L./Cpl.	7.11.17	K. in A.	,,
HALLEWELL, J.	612517	Pte.	7.11.17	K. in A.	,,
JACKSON, G. H.	613785	Pte.	7.11.17	K. in A.	,,
SHILSTON, A.	612059	Pte.	7.11.17	K. in A.	,,
WILDS, J. R.	612637	Pte.	7.11.17	K. in A.	,,
EVANS, F. W.	614329	Pte.	7.11.17	W.	,,
SMART, R. G.	614322	Pte.	7.11.17	W.	,,
BACKSHALL, F.	610588	Pte.	7.11.17	W.	,,
BECK, H. L.	610619	Pte.	7.11.17	W.	,,
BENNETT, J. E.	612687	Pte.	7.11.17	W.	,,
BOLTON, J. E.	610800	Pte.	7.11.17	W.	,,
CLARIDGE, A.	610987	Pte.	7.11.17	W.	,,
FLORENCE, H.	611089	Pte.	7.11.17	W.	,,
GOLDRING, W. E.	610378	Pte.	7.11.17	W.	,,
HALL, G. E.	613875	Pte.	7.11.17	W.	,,
HERFORD, J.	610918	Pte.	7.11.17	W.	,,
HINKS, C.	613556	Pte.	7.11.17	W.	,,
HINSLEY, A. T.	610330	Pte.	7.11.17	W.	,,
MASON, L. W.	613811	Pte.	7.11.17	W.	,,
NEAVES, H.	610029	Pte.	7.11.17	W.	,,
NOYES, W. G.	610047	Pte.	7.11.17	W.	,,
POLLOCK, C. S.	614108	Pte.	7.11.17	W.	,,
REEVE, W.	613954	Pte.	7.11.17	W.	,,
ROYAL, A.	612058	Pte.	7.11.17	W.	,,
RUMLEY, W.	612077	Pte.	7.11.17	W.	,,
SKELTON, F. H.	611842	Pte.	7.11.17	W.	,,
SOLOMON, A. I.	612003	Pte.	7.11.17	W.	,,
SORE, S. H. J.	614318	Pte.	7.11.17	W.	,,
SPALDING, H.	610202	L./Cpl.	7.11.17	W.	,,
SPELLER, H. J.	610896	L./Cpl.	7.11.17	W.	,,
VILE, R.	611054	Pte.	7.11.17	W.	,,
WEST, L. G.	611991	Pte.	7.11.17	W.	,,
GOLDSMITH, R.	612508	Pte.	11.11.17	D. of W.	,,
PLANT, G. W.	613361	L./Cpl.	11.11.17	D. of W.	,,
SMART, R. G.	614322	Pte.	15.11.17	D. of W.	,,
EVANS, F. W.	614329	Pte.	16.11.17	D. of W.	,,
RYAN, L. E.	611867	L./Cpl.	26.11.17	W.	Nebi Samwil.
SOUSTER, J.	611026	Pte.	26.11.17	W.	,,

Name.	Regtl. No.	Rank.	Date.	Nature of Casualty.	Action.
Whitlock, S.	610257	Pte.	26.11.17	W.	Nebi Samwil.
Cheshire, J.	610924	Sgt.	27.11.17	K. in A.	,,
Firmage, F. G.	614078	Pte.	27.11.17	K. in A.	,,
Paynter, S. W.	613893	Pte.	27.11.17	K. in A.	,,
Coupe, T.	612480	Pte.	27.11.17	W.	,,
Creasey, F. A.	613867	Pte.	27.11.17	W.	,,
Darch, R. J. S.	612747	Pte.	27.11.17	W.	,,
Drury, F. A. V.	612187	L./Cpl.	27.11.17	W.	,,
Duffell, F. R. E.	611972	Pte.	27.11.17	W.	,,
Fickling, O. F.	610595	Cpl.	27.11.17	W.	,,
Green, H. A.	610933	Cpl.	27.11.17	W.	,,
Hardwick, R. C.	611499	Pte.	27.11.17	W.	,,
Jenkins, D.	610380	Cpl.	27.11.17	W.	,,
Johnson, J. P.	614461	Pte.	27.11.17	W.	,,
Pickersgill, H.	612579	Pte.	27.11.17	W.	,,
Rowe, J. L.	611908	Pte.	27.11.17	W.	,,
Birtwhistle, L.	612455	Pte.	27.11.17	W.	,,
Blundell, J. S.	611764	Pte.	27.11.17	W.	,,
Chewtor, J.	610969	Pte.	27.11.17	W.	,,
Cullen, J. A.	613917	Pte.	27.11.17	W.	,,
Geeson, E. L.	611778	Pte.	27.11.17	W.	,,
Godfrey, W. C. T.	614415	Pte.	27.11.17	W.	,,
Harris, N. G.	614092	Pte.	27.11.17	W.	,,
Hide, N. S.	613879	Pte.	27.11.17	W.	,,
Hilton, F. R.	610959	Pte.	27.11.17	W.	,,
Husk, N. J.	610953	Cpl.	27.11.17	W.	,,
Smith, S. C.	612008	Pte.	27.11.17	W.	,,
Stanley, N. J.	612612	Pte.	27.11.17	W.	,,
Davies, J. R.		2/Lieut.	28.11.17	D. of W.	,,
Oakley, F. W.	610864	Pte.	28.11.17	D. of W.	,,
Clapson, H.	612734	Pte.	28.11.17	W.	,,
Laidlow, E.	612544	L./Cpl.	28.11.17	W.	,,
Bencher, G. A.		2/Lieut.	29.11.17	W.	Biddu.
Letchford, R. J.	614276	Pte.	29.11.17	W.	,,
Barnes, J.	613593	Pte.	29.11.17	W.	,,
Deacon, W. J.	613641	Pte.	29.11.17	W.	,,
Hunt, O.	612526	Pte.	29.11.17	W.	,,
Donovan, A.	613869	Pte.	30.11.17	K. in A.	,,
Henderson, J. H.		2/Lieut.	30.11.17	W.	,,
Allen, A. E.	610914	Pte.	30.11.17	W.	,,
Ellery, J. W.	614077	Pte.	30.11.17	W.	,,
Hayball, A. H.	614271	Pte.	30.11.17	W.	,,
Langlois, W. H.	613375	Sgt.	30.11.17	W.	,,
Pitt, G. F.	610613	Pte.	30.11.17	W.	,,
Rushton, A. T.	610596	Pte.	30.11.17	W.	,,
Swanborough, W. G.	611949	Pte.	30.11.17	W.	,,

Name.	Regtl. No.	Rank.	Date.	Nature of Casualty.	Action.
Tizzard, R. A.	611629	Pte.	30.11.17	W.	Biddu.
Wellington, A.	610049	Pte.	30.11.17	W.	,,
Wood, T. E.	613986	Pte.	30.11.17	W.	,,
Colyer, W. C.	611665	Pte.	30.11.17	W.	,,
Prowles, H. A.	613897	Pte.	30.11.17	W.	,,
Sims, F. G.	611736	Cpl.	30.11.17	W.	,,
Goodman, C. C.	614085	Pte.	6.12.17	Died of malaria.	Alexandria.
Ward, F.		Capt.	8.12.17	K. in A.	Jerusalem.
Dowling, A. V.	610720	Sgt.	8.12.17	K. in A.	,,
Deadman, F. J.	611439	Cpl.	8.12.17	K. in A.	,,
Biggs, J.	611929	L./Cpl.	8.12.17	K. in A.	,,
Reynolds, H.	614281	Pte.	8.12.17	K. in A.	,,
Pearce, L. B.	613983	Pte.	8.12.17	K. in A.	,,
Wheeler, A. V.	611369	Pte.	8.12.17	K. in A.	,,
Clapson, H.	612734	Pte.	8.12.17	K. in A.	,,
Colyer, W. C.	611665	Pte.	8.12.17	K in A.	,,
Barnes, E. H.	612451	Pte.	8.12.17	K. in A.	,,
Searles, G. H.	611955	Pte.	8.12.17	K. in A.	,,
Winn, W. H. S.	613939	Pte.	8.12.17	K. in A.	,,
Elvin, J.	613942	Pte.	8.12.17	K. in A.	,,
Reed, A.	611878	Pte.	8.12.17	K. in A.	,,
Brown, F.	612458	Pte.	8.12.17	K. in A.	,,
Williamson, C. S.		Capt.	8.12.17	W.	,,
Tabberner, T. K.		Lieut.	8.12.17	W.	,,
Godward, F. H.		2/Lieut.	8.12.17	W.	,,
Angas, R.		2/Lieut.	8.12.17	W.	,,
Bencher, G. A.		2/Lieut.	8.12.17	W.	,,
Elgood, V. A. A.		Capt.	8.12.17	W.	,,
Radcliffe, C. N.		Lieut.	8.12.17	W.	,,
Toder, E. F.		2/Lieut.	8.12.17	W.	,,
Hutchings, T.	610718	Pte.	8.12.17	W.	,,
Webber, C. F.	610811	Pte.	8.12.17	W.	,,
Hutchinson, C.	614472	Pte.	8.12.17	W.	,,
Adams, W.	611509	Pte.	8.12.17	W.	,,
Jacobs, J.	613988	Pte.	8.12.17	W.	,,
Varnes, J.	614431	Pte.	8.12.17	W.	,,
Wallington, C.	610847	Pte.	8.12.17	W.	,,
Aldridge, J.	611069	Pte.	8.12.17	W.	,,
Machon, C. W.	613987	Pte.	8.12.17	W.	,,
Way, W. H. C.	613985	Pte.	8.12.17	W.	,,
Allen, W. V. M.	614061	Pte.	8.12.17	W.	,,
Arnold, S.	611057	Pte.	8.12.17	W.	,,
Bearfield, W.	611986	Pte.	8.12.17	W.	,,
Bethell, T. J.	610195	L./Sgt.	8.12.17	W.	,,
Blyth, W.	612470	Pte.	8.12.17	W.	,,

Name.	Regtl. No.	Rank.	Date.	Nature of Casualty.	Action.
Brookes, J. J.	613973	Pte.	8.12.17	W.	Jerusalem.
Buck, S. H.	614328	Pte.	8.12.17	W.	,,
Chaplet, F.	610967	Pte.	8.12.17	W.	,,
Charing, J.	613977	Pte.	8.12.17	W.	,,
Curtis, G. T.	613976	Pte.	8.12.17	W.	,,
Davies, H. G.	610903	Pte.	8.12.17	W.	,,
Davis, A. G.	611760	Pte.	8.12.17	W.	,,
Chad, G. W.	613678	Pte.	8.12.17	W.	,,
Fairbrother, W.	612506	Pte.	8.12.17	W.	,,
Hammond, H.	611989	Pte.	8.12.17	W.	,,
Harris, J.	611752	Pte.	8.12.17	W.	,,
Hedges, G. A.	614272	Pte.	8.12.17	W.	,,
Howard, S. W.	613530	L./Cpl.	8.12.17	W.	,,
Hull, W.	614416	Pte.	8.12.17	W.	,,
Hurlock, W. A.	611723	Pte.	8.12.17	W.	,,
Melvin, F. G.	610055	Pte.	8.12.17	W.	,,
Miller, A. G.	614102	Pte.	8.12.17	W.	,,
Nolan, E.	612565	Pte.	8.12.17	W.	,,
Palmer, H. J.	611860	Pte.	8.12.17	W.	,,
Porter, A.	613895	Pte.	8.12.17	W.	,,
Price, T. J.	610271	Pte.	8.12.17	W.	,,
Richardson, W. B.	612594	Pte.	8.12.17	W.	,,
Riley, L.	610765	Pte.	8.12.17	W.	,,
Sargent, J. A.	611969	Pte.	8.12.17	W.	,,
Scott, H. R.	610987	Pte.	8.12.17	W.	,,
Sinclair, A.	612598	Pte.	8.12.17	W.	,,
Smith, G.	613443	Pte.	8.12.17	W.	,,
Smith, W.	611771	L./Cpl.	8.12.17	W.	,,
Sprigings, A.	611401	Pte.	8.12.17	W.	,,
Stevens, W. H.	611901	Pte.	8.12.17	W.	,,
Stevenson, F.	613643	Pte.	8.12.17	W.	,,
Stott, E.	612601	Cpl.	8.12.17	W.	,,
Taylor, N. C.	612626	Pte.	8.12.17	W.	,,
Thomas, A. P.	614493	Pte.	8.12.17	W.	,,
Upson, W. G.	611780	Pte.	8.12.17	W.	,,
Wooster, T. W.	611976	Pte.	8.12.17	W.	,,
Anderson, J. L.	611039	Sgt.	8.12.17	W.	,,
Ardley, C. F.	614413	Pte.	8.12.17	W.	,,
Cooper, C.	610759	Pte.	8.12.17	W.	,,
Gordon, J. A.	614086	Pte.	8.12.17	W.	,,
Moir, J.	611125	Pte.	8.12.17	W.	,,
Cox, W. G.	611480	Pte.	8.12.17	W.	,,
Irons, G. E.	612753	L./Cpl.	8.12.17	W.	,,
Notley, P. J.	611727	Cpl.	8.12.17	W.	,,
Tabberner, T. K.		2/Lieut.	9.12.17	D. of W.	,,
Bencher, G. A.		2/Lieut.	9.12.17	D. of W.	,,

Name.	Regtl. No.	Rank.	Date.	Nature of Casualty.	Action.
Jessemey, H. G.	613882	Pte.	10.12.17	D. of W.	Jerusalem.
Setterfield, L.	612622	L./Cpl.	10.12.17	D. of W.	,,
Scott, H. E.	611924	Pte.	11.12.17	D. of W.	,,
Taylor, A. F.	610783	Sgt.	14.12.17	D. of W.	,,
Stone, G. M.	611444	Pte.	16.12.17	D. of W.	,,
Back, A. A.	614063	Pte.	17.12.17	Died.	Macedonia.
Woodier, W.	612636	Pte.	29.12.17	W.	Palestine.
Jarvis, J. W.	612199	Pte.	29.12.17	W.	,,
Chapman, H. W.	613916	Pte.	29.12.17	W.	,,
Barry, J. T.	612448	Pte.	29.12.17	W.	,,
Benmote, A.	614420	Pte.	29.12.17	W.	,,
Walker, A.	612638	Pte.	29.12.17	W.	,,
Heasman, S. A.	614309	Pte.	29.12.17	W.	,,
Bowers, J. A.	611271	Pte.	29.12.17	W.	,,
Ball, W. S.	611028	Pte.	29.12.17	W.	,,
Gower, L. G.	611678	Pte.	29.12.17	W.	,,
Broadey, C.	614465	Pte.	29.12.17	W.	,,
Bevan, F.	610131	Pte.	29.12.17	W.	,,
Cotterell, B. G.	613743	Pte.	29.12.17	W.	,,
Coleman, B.	610974	Pte.	29.12.17	W.	,,
Duke, J. E.	611029	L./Cpl.	29.12.17	W.	,,
Bridger, W. V.	610208	Sgt.	29.12.17	W.	,,
Lynch, C. K.	613274	L./Cpl.	29.12.17	W.	,,
Rogers, W.	611695	Pte.	29.12.17	W.	,,
Roberts, C. J.	355029	Pte.	30.12.17	Drowned at sea.	
Anderson, H.	355170	Pte.	30.12.17	Drowned at sea.	
Cooley, J. W.	355034	Pte.	30.12.17	Drowned at sea.	
Anderson, J. H.	612107	Pte.	7.1.18	W.	,,
Heasman, S. A.	614308	Pte.	20.1.18	D. of W.	,,
Self, W.	611091	Pte.	17.2.18	W.	,,
Hood, G. B.		2/Lieut.	19.2.18	K. in A.	,,
Brunker, H. W. C.	610320	Sgt.	19.2.18	W.	Jericho Road.
Cooper, A.	612475	Pte.	19.2.18	W.	,,
Codling, R. E.	611896	Pte.	19.2.18	W.	,,
Nightingale	614451	Pte.	19.2.18	W.	,,
Stewart, H. P.	612954	Pte.	19.2.18	W.	,,
Tennant, N. R. D.		Capt.	20.2.18	W.	Talat ed Dumm.
Gardiner, A.		Lieut.	20.2.18	W. D. of W. 26.3.18.	,,

Name.	Regtl. No.	Rank.	Date.	Nature of Casualty.	Action.
Barnes, J.	613583	Cpl.	20.2.18	K. in A.	Talat ed Dumm.
Ramus, A.	612859	Pte.	20.2.18	K. in A.	,,
Roberts, R. W.	611859	Pte.	20.2.18	K. in A.	,,
Staples, J. T.	612613	Pte.	20.2.18	D. of W.	,,
Birtwhistle, L.	612455	Pte.	20.2.18	W.	,,
Bowman, S. H.	611075	L./Cpl.	20.2.18	W.	,,
Colla, W.	610940	Pte.	20.2.18	W.	,,
Fangar, F. A.	610282	L./Sgt.	20.2.18	W.	,,
Hurcomb, F. G.	611058	Sgt.	20.2.18	W.	,,
Lucas, G. V.	610947	Pte.	20.2.18	W.	,,
Masters, A. S.	353159	Pte.	20.2.18	W.	,,
Moore, F. A.	611002	Pte.	20.2.18	W.	,,
Pearce, A. H.	351849	Pte.	20.2.18	W.	,,
Sargent, A. J.	614283	Pte.	20.2.18	W.	,,
Webb, W. J.	611348	Pte.	20.2.18	W.	,,
Bailey, C.	610755	Pte.	20.2.18	W.	,,
Collins, E.	354823	Pte.	20.2.18	W.	,,
Gilham, J.	610960	Pte.	20.2.18	W.	,,
Kelland, E. J.	614097	Pte.	20.2.18	W.	,,
McDonald, E. W.	610937	Pte.	20.2.18	W.	,,
Meddick, A. B.	610742	Pte.	20.2.18	W.	,,
Munday, F. H.	612556	L./Cpl.	20.2.18	W.	,,
Pooley, J. F.	612139	Pte.	20.2.18	W.	,,
Severs, H.	612607	Pte.	20.2.18	W.	,,
White, J. T.	353255	Pte.	20.2.18	W.	,,
Baker, F.	612446	Cpl.	20.2.18	W.	,,
Closier, S.	610941	Pte.	20.2.18	W.	,,
Cornish, C.	611631	L./Cpl.	20.2.18	W.	,,
Griggs, L.	610919	Pte.	20.2.18	W.	,,
Kirkham, W.	612542	Pte.	20.2.18	W.	,,
Manning, A.	354984	Pte.	20.2.18	W.	,,
Monk, M. W.	610258	Pte.	20.2.18	W.	,,
Neather, W. H.	612056	Pte.	20.2.18	W.	,,
Salter, E. C.	611210	Pte.	20.2.18	W.	,,
Tasker, A. E.	611287	Pte.	20.2.18	W.	,,
Wincote, W. W.	613966	Pte.	20.2.18	W.	,,
Hayball, A. H.	614271	Pte.	20.2.18	W. (2nd occasion)	,,
Jarvis, J. W.	612199	Pte.	20.2.18	W. (2nd occasion)	,,
Watson, T.	612646	Pte.	21.2.18	D. of W.	,,
Anderson, J. H.	612107	Pte.	22.2.18	D. of W.	,,
Sykes, A.	611068		4.3.18	Died of sickness.	,,
Beresford, S.	612468	Pte.	5.3.18	W. (accident)	Jordan Valley.
Jones, E. I.		2/Lieut.	22.3.18	K. in A.	First Jordan.

Name.	Regtl. No.	Rank.	Date.	Nature of Casualty.	Action.
Pitt, G. F.	610613	Sgt.	22.3.18	K. in A.	First Jordan.
Hobbs, H. J.	613054	Sgt.	22.3.18	K. in A.	,,
Sims, F. G.	611736	Cpl.	22.3.18	K. in A.	,,
Woodman, E.	610797	L./Cpl.	22.3.18	K. in A.	,,
Fincher, W. J.	614316	Pte.	22.3.18	K. in A.	,,
Clark, C.	614324	Pte.	22.3.18	K. in A.	,,
Sore, S. H. J.	614318	Pte.	22.3.18	K. in A.	,,
Wooster, T. W.	611976	Pte.	22.3.18	K. in A.	,,
Putland, W.	611589	Pte.	22.3.18	K. in A.	,,
Bigland, W.	612454	Pte.	22.3.18	K. in A.	,,
Crellin, E.	612486	Pte.	22.3.18	K. in A.	,,
Pratt, C. H.	612574	Pte.	22.3.18	K. in A.	,,
Ellery, J. W.	614077	Pte.	22.3.18	K. in A.	,,
Crane, C. V.	613865	Pte.	22.3.18	K. in A.	,,
Betts, W. F.	614447	Pte.	22.3.18	K. in A.	,,
Golding, P. V.	614458	Pte.	22.3.18	K. in A.	,,
Watts, H. J.	354451	Pte.	22.3.18	K. in A.	,,
Smith, J. H.	353141	Pte.	22.3.18	K. in A.	,,
Arnold, E. W.	354113	Pte.	22.3.18	K. in A.	,,
Bradley, H. T.	612673	Pte.	22.3.18	K. in A.	,,
Taylor, A. E.	613494	Pte.	22.3.18	K. in A.	,,
Smith, H. G.	613955	Pte.	22.3.18	W.	,,
Angel, A.	610954	Pte.	22.3.18	W.	,,
Blackburn, C. W.	611619	Pte.	22.3.18	W.	,,
Brown, J. W.	614448	Pte.	22.3.18	W.	,,
Channing, G.	611413	Pte.	22.3.18	W.	,,
Dagger, H.	610027	Pte.	22.3.18	W.	,,
Dancy, W. S.	610585	Cpl.	22.3.18	W.	,,
Dawson, J. H.	612493	Cpl.	22.3.18	W.	,,
Digman, G. W.	354552	Pte.	22.3.18	W.	,,
Drew, H.	612490	Pte.	22.3.18	W.	,,
Fleming, G.	613666	Pte.	22.3.18	W.	,,
Forss, H. J.	610984	L./Cpl.	22.3.18	W.	,,
Glascoe, E.	611668	Pte.	22.3.18	W.	,,
Goodbody, E.	353265	Pte.	22.3.18	W.	,,
Holman, E.	612525	Pte.	22.3.18	W.	,,
Johnson, J. J. J.	354969	Pte.	22.3.18	W.	,,
Jones, E.	612538	Pte.	22.3.18	W.	,,
Knott, J. W.	355033	Pte.	22.3.18	W.	,,
Lang, C.	614502	Pte.	22.3.18	W.	,,
Lloyd, T. J.	610530	Sgt.	22.3.18	W.	,,
Moy, J. G.	354975	Pte.	22.3.18	W.	,,
Neaves, H.	610029	Pte.	22.3.18	W.	,,
Richards, J.	610405	Pte.	22.3.18	W.	,,
Sibley, C.	610905	Pte.	22.3.18	W.	,,
Smith, W.	611771	L./Cpl.	22.3.18	W.	,,

Name.	Regtl. No.	Rank.	Date.	Nature of Casualty.	Action.
Snelling, G.	613951	Pte.	22.3.18	W.	First Jordan.
Tolhurst, C. J.	612624	Pte.	22.3.18	W.	,,
Whiteley, R.	611353	Pte.	22.3.18	W.	,,
Williams, W.	612182	Pte.	22.3.18	W.	,,
Franklin, R.	613735	Pte.	22.3.18	W.	,,
Berry, A.	613860	Pte.	22.3.18	W.	,,
Ward, F.	614287	Pte.	3.4.18	D. of W.	Palestine.

PALESTINE (SECOND JORDAN ACTION).

Name.	Regtl. No.	Rank.	Date.	Nature of Casualty.	Action.
Gambell, D. C.		Lieut.	30.4.18	K. in A.	Second Jordan.
McHardy, S. J.		2/Lieut.	30.4.18	K. in A.	,,
Franklin, J.	611078	Pte.	30.4.18	K. in A.	,,
Phillips, R. A.	610180	Dmr.	30.4.18	K. in A.	,,
Perry, C.	610975	Cpl.	30.4.18	K. in A.	,,
Simpson, S.	612603	Pte.	30.4.18	K. in A.	,,
Ansell, F. A.	611438	Pte.	30.4.18	K. in A.	,,
Spalding, H.	610202	L./Cpl.	30.4.18	K. in A.	,,
Milne, G.	613679	L./Cpl.	30.4.18	K. in A.	,,
Manning, A.	354984	Pte.	30.4.18	K. in A.	,,
Cox, W. G.	611480	Pte.	30.4.18	K. in A.	,,
Cullen, J. A.	613917	Pte.	30.4.18	K. in A.	,,
Scammell, C. R., D.C.M.	610276	Pte.	30.4.18	K. in A.	,,
Websdale, H.	11352	Pte.	30.4.18	K. in A.	,,
Strawson, G. R. (M.M.)	612602	Pte.	30.4.18	K. in A.	,,
Hebbert, V.	612522	Pte.	30.4.18	K. in A.	,,
Dear, A. G.	614165	Pte.	30.4.18	Missing.	,,
Beamish, H. C.	610562	Cpl.	30.4.18	Missing.	,,
Fry, T. H., D.C.M.	610386	Sgt.	30.4.18	Missing.	,,
Mallinson, J. S.	612549	Pte.	30.4.18	Missing.	,,
Ryan, L. E.	611867	Pte.	30.4.18	Missing.	,,
Rogers, W. B.	G92959	Pte.	30.4.18	Missing.	,,
Popham, F. (Medaille Militaire)	611088	L./Cpl.	30.4.18	Wounded and Missing.	,,
Robinson, C. J.	612809	Pte.	30.4.18	Wounded and Missing.	,,
Surridge, J.	G57153	Pte.	30.4.18	Missing.	,,
Smith, W.	612752	L./Cpl.	30.4.18	W.	,,
Speed, H. C.	610262	L./Cpl.	30.4.18	W.	,,
Stevenson, G. H.	354984	Pte.	30.4.18	W.	,,
Tann, W. J.	611035	Pte	30.4.18	W.	,,
Thorpe, E.	614115	Pte	30.4.18	W.	,,

Name.	Regtl. No.	Rank.	Date.	Nature of Casualty.	Action.
Ulrich, H.	610162	Cpl.	30.4.18	W.	Second Jordan.
Wakefield, A.	612644	Pte.	30.4.18	W.	,,
West, L. G.	611991	Pte.	30.4.18	W.	,,
Williams, J. T.	612647	Pte.	30.4.18	W.	,,
Wiltshire, W. P.	355012	Pte.	30.4.18	W.	,,
Royal, A.	612058	Pte.	30.4.18	W.	,,
Tunbridge, H.	613651	Pte.	30.4.18	W.	,,
Morris, F.	614152	Pte.	30.4.18	W.	,,
Colyer, W. E. P.	614066	Pte.	30.4.18	W.	,,
Hill, A. C.	612756	Pte.	30.4.18	W.	,,
Fowler, G.	610762	Pte.	30.4.18	W.	,,
Boosey, H. E.	611342	Pte.	30.4.18	W.	,,
Greenwood, W.	614084	Pte.	30.4.18	W.	,,
Sharp, W. J.	612702	Pte.	30.4.18	W.	,,
Bowler, G.	611031	Pte.	30.4.18	W.	,,
Sealey, A. H.	611722	Pte.	30.4.18	W.	,,
Allen, W. J. M.	614061	Pte.	30.4.18	W.	,,
Bond, J. W.	G96026	Pte.	30.4.18	W.	,,
Misson, W.	G96043	Pte.	30.4.18	W.	,,
Prest, H.	G96024	Pte.	30.4.18	W.	,,
Underhill, A. E.	G96025	Pte.	30.4.18	W.	,,
Greenway, F.	G57151	Pte.	30.4.18	W.	,,
King, W. W.	612696	Pte.	30.4.18	W.	,,
Kingham, E. W.	611071	L./Cpl.	30.4.18	W.	,,
Lovell, C. S.	610526	Pte.	30.4.18	W.	,,
Maloney, R.	614437	Pte.	30.4.18	W.	,,
Mitchell, W. J.	613887	Pte.	30.4.18	W.	,,
Moy, T. E.	613582	L./Cpl.	30.4.18	W.	,,
Munday, F. H.	612556	L./Cpl.	30.4.18	W.	,,
Myers, L.	612562	Pte.	30.4.18	W.	,,
Naylor, M.	612564	Pte.	30.4.18	W.	,,
Beilson, S. J.	612563	L./Cpl.	30.4.18	W.	,,
Nolan, B.	612566	Pte.	30.4.18	W.	,,
Notley, P. J.	611727	L./Sgt.	30.4.18	W.	,,
Overton, T. J.	353221	Pte.	30.4.18	W.	,,
Palmer, T. W. G.	611959	Pte.	30.4.18	W.	,,
Pearlstein, L.	614395	Pte.	30.4.18	W.	,,
Phillips, H.	611081	Pte.	30.4.18	W.	,,
Pope, W.	610746	Pte.	30.4.18	W.	,,
Preddy, A. G.	611322	Pte.	30.4.18	W.	,,
Porter, A.	613895	Pte.	30.4.18	W.	,,
Price, T. J.	610271	Pte.	30.4.18	W.	,,
Priest, E. E.	613984	Pte.	30.4.18	W.	,,
Pritchett, L.	610446	Pte.	30.4.18	W.	,,
Quigley, E. E.	613594	Pte.	30.4.18	W.	,,
Redden, G. J.	612590	Pte.	30.4.18	W.	,,

Name.	Regtl. No.	Rank.	Date.	Nature of Casualty.	Action.
Reynolds, J.	611032	Pte.	30.4.18	W.	Second Jordan.
Ricketts, F. E.	613826	L./Cpl.	30.4.18	W.	,,
Robinson, C. J.	612809	Pte.	30.4.18	W.	,,
Russell, A.	611952	Pte.	30.4.18	W.	,,
Scattergood, W.	612035	Pte.	30.4.18	W.	,,
Shadbolt, J. L.	612616	Pte.	30.4.18	W.	,,
Shepherd, W.	612609	Pte.	30.4.18	W.	,,
Silbertton, L.	611988	Pte.	30.4.18	W.	,,
Planchat, G. F. A.		2/Lieut.	30.4.18	W.	,,
Walker, L. J.		2/Lieut.	30.4.18	W.	,,
Egerton, P. G.		Capt.	30.4.18	W.	,,
Jones, G. E.		2/Lieut.	30.4.18	W.	,,
Remnant, F.		2/Lieut.	30.4.18	W.	,,
Barker, E.	614144	Pte.	30.4.18	W.	,,
Barron	613909	Pte.	30.4.18	W.	,,
Blight, W. H.	613974	Pte.	30.4.18	W.	,,
Boyes, W. S.	612444	L./Sgt.	30.4.18	W.	,,
Broadbent, S.	612466	Sgt.	30.4.18	W.	,,
Brown, J.	612210	Pte.	30.4.18	W.	,,
Burney, F.	613478	Cpl.	30.4.18	W.	,,
Cohen, L.	614070	Pte.	30.4.18	W.	,,
Coote, G.	610836	Pte.	30.4.18	W.	,,
Cundall, T. W.	612483	Pte.	30.4.18	W.	,,
Davis, W. V.	610279	L./Cpl.	30.4.18	W.	,,
Doran, G. R.	610612	Sgt.	30.4.18	W.	,,
Duke, J. E.	611029	L./Cpl.	30.4.18	W.	,,
Edge, J. P. M.	613981	L./Cpl.	30.4.18	W.	,,
Ellis, S. C.	611830	Pte.	30.4.18	W.	,,
Gosnold, H.	611052	Pte.	30.4.18	W.	,,
Gould, W.	613920	Pte.	30.4.18	W.	,,
Gregory, P. B.	612746	Pte.	30.4.18	W.	,,
Hills, C. F. C.	610703	Pte.	30.4.18	W.	,,
Hinds, C. H.	611041	Pte.	30.4.18	W.	,,
Holman, P. D.	613880	Pte.	30.4.18	W.	,,
Holmes, E. J.	611765	L./Cpl.	30.4.18	W.	,,
Hughes, R.	611567	Pte.	30.4.18	W.	,,
Inward, B.	611719	L./Cpl.	30.4.18	W.	,,
Jackson, A.	614423	Pte.	30.4.18	W.	,,
Jeffrey, W. T.	613881	Pte.	30.4.18	W.	,,
Joslin, W. S.	612539	L./Cpl.	30.4.18	W.	,,
Jones, P. G.	610395	Pte.	1.5.18	D. of W.	,,
Bracey, T. W.	612260	Pte.	2.5.18	Missing	,,
Bailey, C.	614450	Pte.	2.5.18	Missing	,,
Coker, F. R.	610283	Pte.	2.5.18	Missing	,,
Crane, H. W.	610549	Sgt.	2.5.18	Missing	,,
Jarvis, J. W.	612199	Pte.	2.5.18	Missing	,,

Name.	Regtl. No.	Rank.	Date.	Nature of Casualty.	Action.
MILLARD, G.	613886	Pte.	2.5.18	Missing	Second Jordan.
WOHLSCHLAGER, H.	610065	Pte.	2.5.18	Missing	,,
LETCHFORD, C. J...	614276	Pte.	2.5.18	W.	,,
SHEARMAN, S. J.	612623	Pte.	9.5.18	D. of W.	,,
HOLMAN, P. D.	613880	Pte.	19.5.18	D. of W.	,,
MANDER, W. A.	613950	Pte.	2.6.18	Died of Dysentery.	,,
WHITE, J. T.	353283	Pte.	3.6.18	W.	Palestine
BENJAMIN, R.	614186	Pte.	8.6.18	W.	,,
BEAVAN, F.	610131	L./Cpl.	5.7.18	Died of Enteric.	,,
SAUNDERS, C. G. A.	613158	Pte.		Missing, believed drowned on s.s. "Aragon."	,,
SNELLIN, H. J.	355013	Pte.		,,	,,
MARSTON, F. G.	352217	Pte.		,,	,,
MEALE, G. A.	351588	Pte.		,,	,,
ANDERSON, J. F.	610904	Pte.	24.7.18	D. of W.	,,
GARBUTT, A. W.	614309	Pte.	28.7.18	Died of Dysentery.	,,
ALDRIDGE, R. A.	613907	Pte.	2.8.18	Missing	Palestine (Nablus Road).
SKITTRALL, C.	612615	L./Cpl.	2.8.18	Missing	,,
CHAPMAN, G. T. A.	614619	Pte.	10.8.18	W.	Palestine.
SMITH, S. G.	611920	Pte.	14.9.18	Died of Dysentery.	,,
FLEMING, G.	613666	Pte.	19.9.18	K. in A.	Palestine (Nahr El Falik).
WOODS, W. E.	614120	Pte.	19.9.18	K. in A.	,,
WOODFORD, R. E...	611964	Pte.	19.9.18	K. in A.	,,
CHAPLET, F	610967	Pte.	19.9.18	K. in A.	,,
PITTS, C.	610388	Pte.	19.9.18	K. in A.	,,
HORN, W. R.	610053	Pte.	19.9.18	K. in A.	,,
THOMAS, J. H.	614317	L./Cpl.	19.9.18	K. in A.	,,
REYNOLDS, A. V. G.	353731	Pte.	19.9.18	K. in A.	,,
FINN, G. H.	353536	Pte.	19.9.18	K. in A.	,,
DUNN, M...	353711	Pte.	19.9.18	W.	,,
HIGHAM, W. A.	615011	Pte.	19.9.18	W.	,,
ALDRIDGE, J.	611069	Pte.	19.9.18	W.	,,
BAGGS, F.	613667	A./Cpl.	19.9.18	W.	,,
BRAGGER, S.	615003	Pte.	19.9.18	W.	,,
BROWN, W.	613913	Pte.	19.9.18	W.	,,
BUSH, J.	610898	Pte.	19.9.18	W.	,,

Name.	Regtl. No.	Rank.	Date.	Nature of Casualty.	Action.
Callan, D.	614939	Pte.	19.9.18	W.	Palestine
Chapman, H. W.	613916	Pte.	19.9.18	W.	(Nahr El
Curtis, G. T.	613976	Pte.	19.9.18	W.	Falik).
Jenkins, D.	610380	Cpl.	19.9.18	W.	,,
Joyes, F. J.	614742	Pte.	19.9.18	W.	,,
Kimber, V.	614585	Pte.	19.9.18	W.	,,
Martindale, W. M.	614775	Pte.	19.9.18	W.	,,
Repton, C. H. G.	611184	Pte.	19.9.18	W.	,,
Kivlochan, F. L.	612674	Pte.	19.9.18	W.	,,
Knight, H.	614095	Pte.	19.9.18	W.	,,
Mandell, J. L.	614650	L./Cpl.	19.9.18	W.	,,
Mansi, J. B.	613781	Pte.	19.9.18	W.	,,
Merry, A.	613571	L./Cpl.	19.9.18	W.	,,
Morris, A. J.	614698	Pte.	19.9.18	W.	,,
Parkin, G. E.	614745	Pte.	19.9.18	W.	,,
Phillips, H.	611081	Pte.	19.9.18	W.	,,
Rawlins, W. J.	614723	Pte.	19.9.18	W.	,,
Rosamond, R.	613660	Pte.	19.9.18	W.	,,
Sanderson, C. H.	613902	Pte.	19.9.18	W.	,,
Cheeseman	610823	Pte.	19.9.18	W.	,,
Mortlock, C.	614947	Pte.	19.9.18	W.	,,
Challis, P.	611992	Pte.	19.9.18	W.	,,
Sargent, A. J.	614283	Pte.	19.9.18	W.	,,
Smith, H. E. B.	610816	Pte.	19.9.18	W.	,,
Spinks, A. H.	612618	Pte.	19.9.18	W.	,,
Spurge, G. C.	613963	Pte.	19.9.18	W.	,,
Webber, F. J.	611063	Pte.	19.9.18	W.	,,
Welton, E. C.	614967	Pte.	19.9.18	W.	,,
Whitlock, S.	610257	Pte.	19.9.18	W.	,,
Worrall, T.	614997	Cpl.	19.9.18	W.	,,
Wright, W.	612709	Pte.	19.9.18	W.	,,
Hinks, C.	613556	Pte.	19.9.18	W.	,,
Morris, T. C. S.		2/Lieut.	19.9.18	W.	,,
Tills, H. S.	614632	Sgt.	19.9.18	W.	,,
Campbell, R.	G51533	Pte.	19.9.18	W.	,,
Cohen, A.	G57154	Pte.	19.9.18	W.	,,
Sullivan, J.	G7135	Pte.	19.9.18	W.	,,
Edminson, C.	G92999	Pte.	19.9.18	W.	,,
Remnant, F.		2/Lieut.	19.9.18	W.	,,
Chappell, S. J. A. S.	57209	Pte.	19.9.18	W.	,,
Pearce, A. H.	351849	Pte.	21.9.18	D. of W.	,,
Dunn, M.	353711	Pte.	4.10.18	D. of W.	,,
Egerton, P. G.		Capt.	18.10.18	D. of W. (wounded 30.4.18)	,,
Brazier, H. J.	611834	Pte.	10.10.18	Died of Malaria.	,,
Williams, Z.	354778	Pte.	12.10.18	Do.	,,

Name.	Regtl. No.	Rank.	Date.	Nature of Casualty.	Action.
PAGE, B. C.	612162	Pte.	12.10.18	Died of Malaria.	Palestine (Nahr El Falik).
HIGHAM, W. A.	615011	Pte.	22.10.18	D. of W.	,,
KINGSBURY, A. S.	614691	Pte.	31.10.18	Died of Pneumonia.	,,
HUTCHINSON, C.	614472	Pte.	1.11.18	Died of Dysentery.	,,
CARTER, A. J.	L17636	Pte.	25.11.18	Died of Pneumonia.	Egypt.
MILLS, J.	350999	Pte.	3.12.18	Ditto.	,,
GILLMAN, J. W.	612676	Pte.	7.12.18	Ditto.	,,
WALLACE, C. H.	614564	Pte.	10.12.18	Ditto.	,,
SCOTT, H. R.	610897	Pte.	6.1.19	D.	,,
PEARLSTEIN, L.	614395	Pte.	8.1.19	D.	,,
HURLOCK, W. G.	611723	Pte.	9.1.19	D.	,,
HOLMES, E. J.	615217	Pte.	9.1.19	D.	,,
ROSAMOND, T. B.	613386	Pte.	9.1.19	D.	,,
WATSON, W. R.	614532	Pte.	11.1.19	D.	,,
BLACKMORE, E. C.	614653	Pte.	22.1.19	D.	,,
TATNER, G.	614909	Pte.	31.1.19	D.	,,
WILKINSON, A.	612634	Pte.	1.2.19	D.	,,
BASSINGTON, J. A.	611412	Pte.	10.2.19	D.	..
BURTON, F. L. N.	614886	Pte.	18.2.19	D.	,,
BEAVEN, C.	611635	Pte.	8.5.19	Drowned.	,,
COLLA, W.	610940	Pte.	8.5.19	Drowned.	,,
GREENWOOD, W.	617350	Pte.	—	Killed (accident).	Aleppo, Syria.

MISSING—DEATH ACCEPTED.

The names of the undermentioned N.C.O.'s and men which appear in the above lists as "MISSING" were later included in the Casualty Lists as "DEATH ACCEPTED."

Name.	Regtl. No.	Rank.		Date.
FRY, T. H.	610386	Sgt.	Missing.	30.4.18
BEAMISH, H. C.	610562	Cpl.	Missing.	30.4.18
DEAR, A. G.	614165	Pte.	Missing.	30.4.18
MALLINSON, J. S.	612549	Pte.	Missing.	30.4.18
RYAN, A. E.	611867	Pte.	Missing.	30.4.18
ROGERS, W. B.	615316	Pte.	Missing.	30.4.18
POPHAM, F.	611088	L./Cpl.	Missing.	30.4.18
ROBINSON, C. J.	612809	Pte.	Missing.	30.4.18
SURRIDGE, J.	615317	Pte.	Missing.	30.4.18
BAILEY, C.	612456	Pte.	Missing.	2.5.18
BRACEY, T. W.	614260	Pte.	Missing.	2.5.18
JARVIS, J. W.	612199	Pte.	Missing.	2.5.18
ALDRIDGE, R. A.	613907	Pte.	Missing.	2.8.18

APPENDIX II.

HONOURS AND AWARDS.

DISTINGUISHED SERVICE ORDER.
Lt.-Col. D. C. SWORD.
Lt.-Col. A. E. NORTON (2/18th attached).
Major W. M. CRADDOCK (2/20th attached).

BAR TO MILITARY CROSS.
Capt. C. F. ASHDOWN.
Capt. C. N. RADCLIFFE.

MILITARY CROSS.
Capt. C. F. ASHDOWN.
Capt. P. M. BENDALL.
Lt. G. A. L. DUMPHY.
Capt. V. A. A. ELGOOD.
Capt. N. HOBSON.
2/Lieut. G. E. JONES.
Capt. W. H. F. MACKAY.
Capt. C. N. RADCLIFFE.
Capt. F. WARD.
Major C. S. WILLIAMSON.

CROIX DE GUERRE.
Capt. J. G. L. POMMEROL.

ORDER OF THE NILE.
Capt. P. M. BENDALL.

DISTINGUISHED CONDUCT MEDAL.
Sgt. A. B. FULLER.
Sgt. T. H. FRY.
Sgt. S. F. LANGLEY.
Pte. C. R. SCAMMELL.
Sgt. W. H. LANGLOIS.
R.S.M. W. A. MANNING.

MILITARY MEDAL.

Sgt. J. L. ANDERSON.
Sgt. W. V. BARRETT.
Sgt. T. J. BETHELL.
Sgt. C. H. COLCLOUGH.
Pte. A. C. HARDWICK.
Cpl. W. HARDY.
Pte. J. HERFORD.
Pte. T. HITCHINGS.
L./Cpl. C. J. LAMING.
Cpl. E. MARGRAVE.
Pte. H. PICKERSGILL.
Pte. D. E. RANDALL.
Pte. R. ROBERTS.
L./Cpl. H. C. SPEED.
Pte. G. R. STEVENSON.
Pte. J. TANSEY.

MEDAILLE MILITAIRE.

L./Cpl. F. Popham.

MERITORIOUS SERVICE MEDAL.

R.Q.M.S. (A/R.S.M.) G. A. EARL.

MENTIONED IN DISPATCHES.

Capt. G. E. ANDREAS.
Capt. & Q.M. E. BLEEZE.
Pte. J. S. BLUNDELL
Capt. J. BOWERING.
Capt. T. R. G. BENNETT.
Lieut. G. BROWN.
Lieut. M. N. BUTTENSHAW.
Major W. M. CRADDOCK
  (2/20th, attached 2/19th).
Lieut. A. F. CUOLAHAN
  (2/18th, attached 2/19th).
C.S.M. W. H. DOE.
Sgt. W. W. J. EVERS.
Cpl. W. HARDY (twice).
Lieut. R. H. HEATON.
L./Sgt. E. M. HOARE.
Capt. N. HOBSON.
Sgt. S. F. LANGLEY.
R.S.M. W. A. MANNING.
Lieut. C. MERIFIELD.
Lt.-Col. A. E. NORTON (3 times),
Capt. J. G. L. POMMEROL.
L./Cpl. A. E. PEASLAND.
Lieut. G. F. A. PLANCHAT.
A./R.Q.M.S. S. SQUIRES.
Lt.-Col. D. C. SWORD.
L./Cpl. H. R. TURNER.
Capt. E. F. TODER.
Capt. F. WARD.
Major C. S. WILLIAMSON (twice).

APPENDIX III.

Diary, 1914—1918.

1914.
August .. Formation of 2/19th London Regiment.
September .. Training in Regent's Park.
October .. Moved to White City.

1915.
Jan. 2 .. Moved into billets at Reigate.
" 22 .. Inspection by Lord Kitchener on Epsom Downs.
" 30 .. Issued with Japanese rifles and bayonets.
March 10 .. Issued with equipment.
" 30 .. Moved into billets vacated by 1/19th at St. Albans.
May 10 .. Marched to Ware.
" 11 .. Marched to Bishop's Stortford.
" 12 .. Marched to Coggeshall.
June 26 .. Moved into billets at Braintree.
" 29 .. Brigade Camp at Hatfield Broad Oak.
Oct. 25 .. Moved into billets at Saffron Walden.
Dec. .. Moved into billets at Hertford.
" 22 .. Inspection by General Bulfin.

1916.
Jan. 7 .. Moved into Divisional Camp, Sutton Veney.
June 23 .. Left camp at Sutton Veney. Embarked Southampton for France.
" 24 .. Landed at Havre.
" 25 .. Entrained Havre.
" 26 .. Detrained Petit Houvin. Billets at La Croisette.
" 27 .. Marched to billets at Maizieres.
July 6 .. Relieved 1/5 Seaforth Highlanders on Vimy Ridge.
" 26 .. Tidza crater blown on 2/20th front.
" 28 .. Enemy blew crater (Devon) on 2/19th front.
" 31 .. Enemy raided Duffield crater (2/20th).
Aug. 16 .. 2/20th put up a mine on lip of Grange.
" 30/31 .. 2/19th raided German trenches in front of Lichfield crater.
Oct. 23 .. Relieved by 49th Canadian Infantry, 7th Division. Moved to Mont St. Eloi.
Nov. 1 .. Inspected by Sir Douglas Haig at Berneuil.
" 20 .. Left Ailly Le Haut Clocher, marched to Longpré. Entrained for Marseilles.
" 25 .. Embarked Marseilles on s.s. "Caledonia."

1916.
Dec. 1 .. Disembarked at Salonika. Marched to Dudular camp.
,, 18 .. Marched to Narech.
,, 19 .. ,, ,, Salamanli.
,, 20 .. ,, ,, Sarigol.
,, 22 .. ,, ,, Janes.
,, 23 .. ,, ,, Mihalova.
,, 24 .. ,, ,, Spancova Farm.
,, 25 .. Christmas Day spent at Spancova Farm.
,, 27 .. "B" Company marched to Vardino.

1917.
Jan. 6 .. "A" Company moved to Vardino.
,, 13 .. "C" ,, ,, ,, ,,
Feb. 27 .. Moved from Vardino into support of 65th Brigade. Bivouacked at Caussica.

March 1 .. Blizzard.
,, 8 .. Relieved 9th South Lancs.
,, 18 .. Enemy aircraft bombed 2/19th lines.
,, 19 .. Moved into front line.
,, 26 .. Relieved by 8th South Wales Borderers. Moved to Oreovica.

April 5 .. Enemy aircraft bombed Karasuli.
,, 7 .. Moved to "The Crag."
,, 8 .. "A" Company moved into support of 2/17th in
(Easter Sun.) I sector. "D" Company to Lothian Ravine.
April 24 .. 2/20th raided "The Nose." 2/19th raid on Les Mitrailleuses cancelled.
,, 27 .. Took over I sector (Waggon Hill).

May 17 .. Relieved by Argyle & Sutherland Highlanders. Moved to Mihalova.
,, 29 .. Moved to Bare Hill (Gugunci).

June 2 .. Marched to Amberkoj.
,, 3 .. ,, ,, Narech.
,, 4 .. ,, ,, Dudular.
,, 10 .. Embarked Salonika on s.s. "Minnetonka."
,, 12 .. Disembarked Alexandria.
,, 13 .. Arrived at Ismailia and camped at Moascar.
,, 24 .. Officers' Dinner, Ismailia.

July 5/6 .. Marched to El Ferdan.
,, 7 .. ,, ,, Kantara (Suez Canal).
,, 8 .. Entrained for Deir el Belah.
,, 29 .. Sheik Nuran.
,, 30 .. El Shauth.

Aug. 27 .. Moved to Tel el Fara.

1917.
Oct.	8	..	To Gamli.
,,	20	..	Back to El Shauth.
,,	29	..	Left El Shauth. Night march to Wadi Mirtaba.
,,	30	..	Moved down Wadi Shanag.
,,	31	..	Attack on Beersheba, 180th Bgde. in Divisional Reserve.
Nov.	2	..	Bivouacked 1½ miles S.W. Beersheba.
,,	3	..	Battalion column bombed by enemy aircraft.
,,	5/6	..	Concentration of 74th, 60th and 10th Divisions for attack on Kauwukah (Sheria).
,,	6	..	Battalion attack at Kauwukah.
,,	7	..	Sheria captured.
,,	8	..	Marched to Huj.
,,	11	..	,, ,, Wadi Jemmameh.
,,	12	..	,, ,, Wadi Hesi.
,,	13	..	Returned to Jemmameh.
,,	14	..	Marched to Abu Hareira.
,,	19	..	,, ,, Gaza.
,,	22	..	,, ,, Junction Station, via El Kustine.
,,	23	..	,, ,, Latron.
,,	25	..	Relieved Scottish Rifles in the line at Nebi Samwil.
,,	27	..	Enemy bombardment and attack on 2/19th position at Nebi Samwil.
,,	28	..	Relieved by 2/20th. Moved to Biddu.
,,	30	..	Shelled at Biddu.
Dec.	1	..	(?) Relieved 181st Brigade.
,,	5	..	Relieved by 25th Battalion R.W.F.
,,	6	..	Joined Brigade.
,,	7	..	Concentrated for attack at Kulonieh.
,,	8	..	Attack on defences of Jerusalem (Deir Yesin).
,,	9	..	Surrender of Jerusalem. 180th Brigade attack on Shafat and Tel el Ful.
,,	11	..	General Allenby's entry into Jerusalem. 2/19th provided Guard of Honour.
,,	18	..	Relieved London Irish on Nablus Road.
,,	23	..	London Irish unsuccessfully attacked Khurbet Adaseh.
,,	24	..	Moved to billets in Jerusalem.
,,	25	..	Battalion spent Christmas Day in Jerusalem as Divisional Reserve.
,,	27	..	Enemy counter-attacks on Jerusalem defences beaten off.
,,	28	..	2/19th occupied Whaleback Hill.
,,	29	..	2/19th occupied Tel el Nasbeh; attacked Shab Salah. Capture of Bireh.

1918.
Jan.	3	..	Relieved Cheshires at Er Ram and Jeba.
,,	7	..	Enemy attacks on 2/19th posts at Jeba beaten off.
,,	16	..	Relieved by 2/21st. Billeted in Jerusalem.

1918.

Jan.	19	"Roosters" pantomime.
,,	26	2/19th took over line on Jericho Road (Suffa and White Hill).
Feb.	4	Major Craddock (2/20th) took over temporary command of 2/19th.
,,	19	2/19th concentrated in Wadi Ruabeh for attack on Talat et Dumm; 2/20th captured Arak Ibrahim.
,,	20	2/19th attack on Talat ed Dumm.
,,	21	Advanced to Khan Kakun, overlooking Jordan Valley.
,,	23	Returned to Talat ed Dumm.
March	4	Reconnaissance of Jordan crossings.
,,	20	Left Talat ed Dumm for River Jordan.
,,	21/22	Battalion crossed River Jordan by swimmers and rafts at Makhadet Hajlah. Bridge-head formed.
,,	24	Marched to Ghoraniyeh.
,,	25	Marched to Shunet Nimrin. Bombed by enemy aircraft.
,,	30	Marched to El Howeij bridge (Es Salt road).
April	1	Withdrew to Shunet Nimrin.
,,	2/3	Held Jordan bridge-head. Relieved by Australian Light Horse; marched to Khan Kakun.
,,	7	Bivouacked 1½ miles N.W. Jericho.
,,	14	Withdrew to Talat ed Dumm.
,,	18	Demonstration near River Jordan.
,,	19	Moved to camp on Mount of Olives, Jerusalem.
,,	27	Left camp on Mount of Olives for Second Jordan action.
,,	29/30	Battalion attacked Shunet Nimrin (reached line of caves).
May	2	2/17th, with 16 platoon, "D" Company, 2/19th attacked Shunet Nimrin.
,,	4	Withdrew across Jordan.
,,	6	Returned to Mount of Olives.
,,	7	Moved to Ramallah.
,,	12	Brigade Horse Show.
,,	14	,, Sports Competition.
,,	15	,, Boxing Competition.
,,	24	Moved up Nablus Road to Ain Yebrud.
,,	27	2/17th and 2/20th left Brigade on transfer to France.
,,	29	Relieved 1/4 Cheshires on Sheik Selim and Highgate Ridge (Mezrah esh Sherkiyeh).
Sept.	14	Moved to camp 3 miles W. of Ramleh.
,,	15	,, ,, concealed camp 2 miles N.E. of Jaffa.
,,	16/18	Moved forward to concentration place for final attack. Reached Black Watch Wadi 9 p.m. on Sept. 18th.
,,	19	Attack and crossing of Nahr el Falik. Marched N.E. to Burin.

1918.
Sept. 20 .. Marched to Tul Keram.
" 21 .. Moved to Anebta, 6 miles E. of Tul Keram.
" 22 .. Moved back to Tul Keram.
" 23 .. Moved to Kalkilieh.
" 24 ..   "   " Fejja.
" 30 ..   "   " Mulebbis.

Oct. 6 ..   "   " Sheik Muannis.
" 31 .. Armistice concluded with Turks.

Nov. 9 .. Entrained for Kantara (Egypt).
" 11 .. Armistice with Germany.

Dec. 25 .. Christmas Day spent at Alexandria.

1919.
March 16 .. Left Sidi Bishr for Port Said. Embarked for Beirut *en route* for Homs.
" 24 .. Amalgamated with 2nd Battalion the Leicestershire Regiment.

April 3 .. Moved to Aleppo.

Dec.   ..   "   " Kantara.
" 23 .. Guard of Honour provided for Lord Allenby. This was the last public appearance of 2/19th.
" 25 .. Christmas Day at Kantara.

1920.
February   .. 2/19th Disbanded.

APPENDIX IV.

Diary of Sergeant H. W. Crane, 16 Platoon, "D" Company, 2/19th London Regiment, captured at Shunet Nimrin in the Second Jordan Action on May 2nd, 1918.

No. 16 Platoon, being in support of the 2/17th London, followed up the attacking waves until the plain ended and we came to the base of the hills which in places rose sheer. It was about 2.45 a.m. and we realised that we should soon lose the cover of darkness, so I hurried the platoon on as much as possible. The platoon responded gamely and went for that hill like firemen intent on subduing a flaming house. In fact the impression of climbing a ladder was obvious, so steep and craggy was the hillside. Meanwhile by the aid of a bright moon the Turks were firing at us from the hill crest on our left. The usefulness of this fire was doubled by the showers of splinters which rose from the brittle rocks and caused us some casualties. After some exertion we reached the top and found, as we expected, that the enemy had evacuated his forward trenches, which lined the cliff. Thinking that all was well and that the attacking line was still advancing we advanced to reinforce. The hill top undulated gently, a lucky thing for us.

On our drawing the attention of the 17th officer to a party of men in open order eighty yards in front, he called to them, asking if they were our attackers. We all shouted but there was no answer, so we cautiously advanced. The question was soon decided, for the people opposite dropped down and opened fire on us. We were soon returning their fire, taking advantage of an undulation that offered cover. This brisk exchange continued some time and we were helped by the platoon Lewis Gun, which came into action in fine style and helped to keep back the Turks, who, in the gathering daylight, saw our numbers and began to advance in superior force.

Our casualty list was growing. To this day I do not know its full extent but I saw two killed and several wounded, which reduced us to about twelve or fourteen strong. We realised that the attackers had either withdrawn, though not through us, or lost their direction in the darkness; in any case we were in a very unenviable position. We withdrew fighting, exchanging bombs with the enemy and putting up an excellent resistance. Getting down that hill was an awful rough and tumble, the sharp rocks taking bloody toll of our bare knees. We naturally got scattered. Some made a bolt for the open plain and came under a murderous fire from the cliffs above us. Others came with me to the 17th Coy. H.Q., which had been established in a low cave at the foot of the hill. Coy. H.Q. was still there and included a 2/17th officer (Mr. Pearson), signallers, stretcher-bearers and wounded. I sat down and decided that my men should make a bee-line for the bushes which dotted the plain. They could do this singly in different directions when the heavy fire from above died down.

There were in the cave seven of my platoon.

The question of getting the wounded away also occupied our attention. This indeed seemed hopeless as one was a foot wound and there was also a sprained ankle.

Things then happened very suddenly and we realised with consternation that the Turks had followed us down the hill, and having enfiladed us from the side and covered us from above, were calling on us to surrender. Resistance was useless and we were soon trailing reluctantly up the hill again, surrounded by jubilant Turks. They lost no time in helping themselves to our valises which contained our rations and "battle order." The whole party, numbering twenty, were taken to the Turkish Divisional Commander, an excellent man who shewed us the greatest consideration. He immediately ordered the wounded to hospital and had a tent erected for the remainder. Mr. Pearson, I believe, shared a tent with a Turkish staff-officer next to the general's own. We were given a meal of meat with rice, and were guarded in our tent day and night.

May 5th.—We remained under guard in the tent until the 5th, during which time we were questioned. We were made to understand that we were not obliged to answer any question. Personally I found that they seemed to know everything worth knowing, for they suggested the correct answer when I refused it. I was greatly pleased with their praise of our 60th Division, how it had steadily pushed back their left since Beersheba, also its splendid fighting qualities. We were amply fed with meat, rice and sheets of dried apricot. Soon after dark we began our trek along the Es Salt road, Mr. Pearson bringing up the rear on a white pony lent him by our friend the general who handed round his cigarettes among us at parting. About 10 p.m. we halted at what seemed to be a field hospital. Here we had an excellent supper and a very improvised concert with some wounded Turkish officers, each side giving turn and turn about. I think we won the palm for sheer noise with "Good By-ee."

May 6th.—At 6 a.m. we were put on board iron-wheeled German lorries and taken to Es Salt. The road in a very bad state of repair. Our iron wheels gave us a fearful bumping. We travelled along the side of the Nimrin gorge passing a derelict British Red Cross ambulance, left behind after the first raid. The gorge is thick with verdure. Its rushing stream is bordered with trees and its sides a mass of pink hollyhocks. We reached Es Salt 10 a.m. Here were several wounded Australians, one huge chap a pitiable sight in his bleeding and exhausted condition, just able to stand with the help of a diminutive Turk. Couldn't get to them. We were incarcerated in a stone chamber and given a loaf of their war bread and a pitcher of water.

May 8th.—We were questioned by both Turkish and German intelligence officers, who worked apart and seemed great rivals. The Turkish methods were absurdly amateurish and caused some merriment. Both parties before pumping us bribed us with eggs, raisins, etc., but their kindness was misplaced, for we had a much needed feed at the expense of very negligible information. The German was, I think, a Lieutenant Heineman who spoke very good English and lived in Balham before the war. We soon realised that the Germans were virtual dictators and that the Turks resented that fact.

May 10th.—Proceeded by lorry to Amman. Trail of British bully tins along the road, left from last raid. Arrived at Amman 1 p.m. After a last longing look at the towers of the Mount of Olives, just visible in the dim distance, we were taken to the station and entrained. At 9 p.m. we left for Damascus.

May 11th.—Journey north uninteresting. Being crammed in a metre gauge truck with Bedouins did not improve my powers of observation. Snow-capped Hermon in view. Country very flat. Plenty of grain of a poor quality.

May 12th.—Arrived at Damascus 5 p.m. and were marched all through the middle of the city and lodged in large building already full of civilian prisoners and internees. The place was infamous and unfit for animals. Vermin was thick upon the walls and the smell was atrocious.

May 13th.—To our great relief we were taken to Hamidiyeh Barracks and placed in an airy upper room. Twice a day we were brought a concoction of boiled grass, pea and bean pods and olive oil. Our kit being stolen and spoons gone, we ravenously scooped the mess up with our hands. A small loaf, weighing ½ lb., and this hogs' food was our daily subsistence for four days. Two of our number went into hospital.

May 17th.—I wrote to the Spanish Consul of Damascus, having heard that he has charge of a relief fund for British subjects.

May 19th.—The Consul arrived and gave each man $T£3$, depreciated value about 12s. A Greek interpreter, who seemed as much a prisoner as ourselves, was quickly commissioned to buy food for us. We had to trust someone. Luckily he turned up trumps and arrived back loaded with bread, goats' cheese and garlic. Numerous vendors, attracted by our new wealth, clamoured for admittance, but only a few who handsomely tipped our coal-black Nubian guard were lucky enough to get in.

May 21st.—Entrained at 2 p.m. and left for Aleppo, passing through the splendid scenery of Anti-Lebanon.

May 22nd.—Passed Rayak, a large depôt, at mid-day. The profusion of roses here deserves mention. We could smell their scent for miles. Reached Aleppo at 6 p.m. It is a large city in the centre of which rises a great mound surmounted by the citadel. We were taken to the Artillery Barracks, where the vermin kept us awake all night.

May 23rd.—In our room, or rather cellar, are Arabs, Indians, Serbs, Russians, Tunisians, Armenians and Turks. An awful babel fills the place. Twice daily we receive a good meat stew and two small loaves like buns.

May 24th.—The Spanish Consul of Aleppo arrived, without being asked this time, and distributed money, clothing, tea, sugar, soap and razors. An elegant Turk, who had a contract for showing prisoners round Aleppo, failed in his efforts to extract money from us. We had learnt our lesson in Damascus and wisely spent our funds on food only.

May 31st.—Entrained at 8 a.m. and left Aleppo for some prisoners' depôt further north.

June 1st.—Detrained at Kelebek where we found some 100 British prisoners at work on the Bagdad Railway. From Kelebek onwards the line is narrow gauge. All prisoners are employed broadening the gauge to Belemedik, 30 miles north. A tattered sergeant regaled us with "coffee," really burnt corn, crushed and boiled.

June 2nd.—No work on Sundays. Wrote home for first time since capture.

June 6th.—A German company has the contract for broadening the gauge. We were entirely handed over to the Germans, who soon had us working under Herr Schmidt, the foreman. Each man should receive $1\frac{1}{4}$ kilogrammes of meat per week, equal to about 7 ozs. per day. We seldom got that amount. Also a small loaf of bread which often went bad by sundown, and peas, or horse-beans, which never boiled soft. This diet soon began to play havoc with our digestions.

The prisoners' hospital is always full. It is situated at Dorak, a mile away, and fortunately boasts an English doctor who was captured at Kut el Amara. He recommends men for convalescent treatment at Affiun Kara Hissar. The number of deaths occurring there does not speak very well for the treatment.

We begin work at 5 a.m. and work until 6 p.m., with a dinner break from 11 a.m. to 1.30 p.m. The work consists of transferring earth from a cutting to an embankment. This is done with small tip-up trucks.

Kelebek has a small bazaar where trashy goods and eatables may be had in exchange for much paper money. The bazaar folk were anxious to barter for any English article we possessed.

Our hut in a filthy state. Vermin everywhere.

Saturday, June 22nd.—Whilst coupling up two trucks I trapped my hand between them. To Dorak Hospital. Out again next day to make room for fever patients.

July 5th.—Received £3 each from home government, also food, mostly potatoes and rice.

Sunday, July 7th.—Seventy of us moved north to Kusuluk. Owing to our failing health our output decreasing. The German contractor has replaced us with a large party of healthy Gurkha prisoners.

On arrival at Kusuluk a large consignment of parcels distributed, one between two. They mostly belong to dead prisoners.

July 8th.—I have a party of fifteen who work at Kusuluk station unloading and loading cement, etc. A large tunnel is almost completed for the broad gauge. Weather hot and unhealthy. Busied myself building a hut of stolen wood and branches.

Sunday, July 21st.—Two of my party are in hospital and six are sick. We get a daily dose of quinine. So far I seem to keep well.

August 4th.—I left Kusuluk and went to Kelebek convalescent hut with a touch of fever.

August 8th.—All British left Kusuluk and Kelebek and entrained south to Adana, a big agricultural centre on the broad gauge.

August 12th.—We are now under the Turks again loading and unloading wood in the station. The freedom allowed us by the Germans is now a thing of the past. A Turkish guard follows us everywhere. We receive a good loaf of bread and bowl of thin porridge each morning. In the evening a weak broth containing pieces of lights and bean pods. Thank God we get a little help from home.

Sunday, August 18th.—I went into Adana Hospital with influenza. I had already had the worst of it in camp so soon mended. Little food there. Our clothes were taken from us and "baked." This happened before we entered the hospital so that we were obliged to traverse one of the main thoroughfares of the city in our shirts only.

August 20th.—During the last three days two of our comrades have died in this hospital, one of my own platoon. It is to the disgrace of the Germans that we were handed over to the Turks. Hospital staffed with inexperienced Armenian nurses. Our doctor is an Arab who studied in London. He is fond of chatting to us about his stay in England and helps cheer things up a little. Food consists of tea, rice, bread and a species of junket or "leban" made of soured milk.

August 22nd.—Out of hospital. Found a small inn and sat in the crowded veranda where everyone seemed to be eating large stuffed gherkins. Did not fancy them, so had a small freshwater fish for which I paid 15 piastres.

August 30th.—The S.M. (M.G.C.) in charge of British evaded the sentry and had a day in Adana. He was brought back under guard and lodged in a stable among the donkeys for 48 hours.

September 16th.—In hospital again with touch of dysentery.

September 23rd.—Out again feeling very weak.

October 18th.—Life is too hopelessly humdrum to keep a diary. We have had a diversion to-day however. Train loads of German and Turkish wounded, crowded to the roofs, have been passing through. Our guards wear an anxious look but refuse to give news. The debris of aeroplanes, guns, etc., speak for themselves though, and we conclude that Allenby is giving them hell down south. We work in relays day and night loading tree-trunks, both whole and ready split for the engines (there is little or no coal available) which are being overworked to evacuate the troops and material. The German staff are making frenzied efforts to keep the line clear, but blocks keep occurring. Eventually we learned from an Armenian of the British advance to Damascus and Aleppo and the great probability of an early peace with Turkey. Even the Germans begin to admit this and in their headlong rush north leave us bread and clothing and forget to scowl.

October 21st.—We have heard from the friendly Armenian of the Allied wedge in Bulgaria, which explains the German hurry.

October 22nd.—Fearing our recapture, the Turks are sending us north. Whole party left Adana mid-day, crammed into one truck, some having to sit with their legs dangling out of the doors. Accident through careless shunting. A truck had been left too near the points. There was a grazing collision which caught the legs of the men at the door before they could get in. Train quickly brought to a standstill and injured men removed. One of them was our guard, a Turkish Ombashi. His legs were so fearfully injured that he died shortly afterwards. In our weakened state this accident reacted upon all of us, I for one felt ill for the rest of the journey. Silent and depressed we jolted on into the interior of Asia Minor over the now finished broad gauge which British prisoners had worked so hard to complete.

October 23rd.—Arrived at Belemedik in the morning, a small town nestling among the Taurus mountains. Pine covered heights overlooked by towering crags. Stayed there all day. Whilst travelling we get a small loaf of bread and nothing else. It is full of straw and nearly chokes one. Unable to procure coal the Turks have ruthlessly cut down their forests for wood to run their railways. For miles the tree-stumps meet the eye and seem to be hurrying past the train in serried ranks as if to escape their degradation beyond the horizon.

October 24th.—Continued our journey and detrained at Bozanti in the evening. No shelter, no rations. For sheer neglect this is the worst yet. Had to work loading wood as usual.

October 25th.—Thirty-two of us still living in the open in drizzling rain, our clothing the shoddiest of rags, mostly fibre cloth full of splinters. Got soaked through. Soon felt the effects, shivers and fever.

October 27th.—We were at last given shelter in a miserable open shed in a filthy yard. The latter was already crowded with camels, horses and many Arabs.

October 29th.—Help at last. Some home parcels and T£1 per man arrived.

November 2nd.—Now that the armistice with Turkey is signed, the Red Crescent authorities have suddenly realised our condition. We were given a fairly good barrack and were able to feel dry again.

November 4th.—No work being done. Our wood-loading days seem to be over. Noticeable improvement in the demeanour of the Turks towards us.

November 6th.—The party left Bozanti and marched to Belemedik. This six-mile march showed me how weak I had become. We had good barracks again.

November 7th.—A large consignment of British parcels released, together with medical comforts. Any food we had been receiving from the Turks now practically ceased. There is a large theatre and cinema here. Needless to say we never miss a programme. We seldom see a German now except a padre who helped us bury a comrade to-day in a large German cemetery. He gave an address in his own language as we stood bareheaded on the bleak hillside.

November 16th.—Inoculated against cholera. Received a letter from home, the first since capture. It is numbered 4; where are the other three? Another of our men died. Doubly tragic now that we are so near repatriation. Our health is rapidly improving, owing chiefly to tinned food from England and the knowledge that our release cannot be delayed much longer. The Union Jack is hoisted over our barrack and we make our presence generally felt in one way or another. Herr Schmidt, the foreman of Kelebek, has put in an appearance and cordially salutes us. Rather different to the gentleman we knew five months ago. We should be moving homewards soon. The railway is choked with traffic.

November 22nd.—All British invited to the commandant's house. Music in the garden by Serbian violinists. The Serbian prisoners have had terrible hardships, having had no country to send them help. The commandant ordered our photos to be taken and sent round little cakes, cigars and cigarettes.

December 2nd.—The French prisoners left for home. British getting restive.

December 8th.—Visited the commandant's house again. Whole party photographed. Cigars and cigarettes in plenty. Farewell concert in the cinema. The Turks are now the most amiable of beings and are delighted to be rid of the Germans. I feel sure they rue the day that they threw in their lot with the central empires.

At 7 p.m. we left Belemedik. Train decorated with Union Jacks, made by the Indian prisoners. Serbians and Russians also on board, all in high spirits (in more senses than one, having got a great deal of raki with them).

December 9th.—Arrived Kelebek 2 a.m. Our engine left us for some unknown reason.

December 10th.—Stranded at Kelebek until 3 p.m. when an engine was at last provided which took us as far as Tarsus where we arrived at 3 p.m. Stayed on train for night.

December 11th.—Learnt that we were to embark at Mersina. Could not wait for a train, so whole party walked there. All became thoroughly excited as we came in sight of the sea, especially when we observed a British ship riding at anchor off the port. Mersina is a small town on Gulf of same name. There are evident signs of bombardment from sea or air. We were welcomed by British officers and received the first definite information of the end of the War. We now parted from our captors and their mismanagement and neglect. Shortly after arrival we were counted and embarked on lighters which took us to the troopship "Huntspil." An officer received us on board saying cheerily, "You are on British soil again now boys." The "Huntspil" left Mersina at 4 p.m. and we were soon steaming south. In the gathering darkness we watched the grim receding bulk of the Taurus Mountains with feelings of fervent joy and relief. Most of us turned into our bunks early and slept the soundest sleep for many a night.

December 12th.—Called at Beyrut to disembark Arab and Armenian refugees, mostly women. Voyage resumed 1 p.m. The stewards gathered all the old newspapers in the ship. Spent the evening reading them. Learnt of many great happenings hitherto unknown to us.

December 13th.—Put into Port Said 11 a.m. We remained on board whilst the ship was coaled and began to hope that we should continue on to England.

December 14th.—Landed at 2 p.m. and went to the Transit Camp. Still clothed in our fibre clothing. All looked and felt the most disreputable crowd on earth.

December 16th.—Got rid of our Turkish clothing and had a creosote bath which I shall not forget in a hurry. All were fitted out with a complete kit.

December 24th.—The British residents have taken us under their wing and are giving us a good time. A special diet seems to have been arranged for us, our mess tables are a sight to see. There is a great improvement in the looks of the party already, even the lean, fever-ridden men are beginning to loosen their belts.

December 25th.—Attended service in English church. Thought of our last Christmas when the 2/19th were billeted in Jerusalem, wondering where the Turkish counter-attack was going to fall.

December 26th.—All ex-prisoners of war embarked on s.s "Canberra" for the first stage of our journey home.

December 27th.—Left Port Said. Arrived Taranto, Italy, December 30th.

January 1st, 1919.—We began our long train journey through Italy and France, putting up here and there at a rest camp for the night.

January 8th.—Arrived at Calais.

January 10th.—Embarked on the "Scotia" and crossed to Dover. Entrained to Canterbury P.O.W. repatriation camp.

January 11th.—Two months' furlough. Arrived home 11 p.m.

INDEX.

	PAGE
Abbeville	40
Acq	28
Afule, El	150
Ailly le Haut Clocher	40
Aleppo	156, 157
Alexandria	60, 157
Allenby, General Sir E.	61, 66, 73, 107, 150
Amman	139, 140, 141, 142
Arak Ibrahim	125, 127
Ardzan, Lake	47
Arish, El	75
Arras	22
Ashdown, Capt. C. F.	13, 21, 32, 35, 37, 39, 90, 125, 158
Ashton, Lieut.	82
Aubigny	28
Bantick, Capt. S. H.	8
Barnstormers	133
Barratt, Sergt.	39
Beamish, Cpl.	145
Beersheba	68, 77, 78, 81
Beirut	156, 157
Beit Hannina	117
Beitin (Bethel)	120
Bencher, Lieut.	54, 98
Bendall, Capt. P. M.	13
Bennett, Lieut.	33
Bethlehem	117
Biddu	92, 93
Bilibel, Tel el	143, 145
Bireh	118, 119, 120
Bleeze, Capt. E.	16, 95, 161
Blue Dome Monastery	133, 134
Bois des Alleux	25
Bottomley, Horatio	10
Brown, Durward	4
Brown Hill	118
Bulfin, Gen. E. S.	14, 68, 150

Cairo	61, 69
Carey, Lieut.	13, 120
Carleton, Gen.	42, 74
Carlton Hall, Maj. W. G.	9, 16
Caussica	53
Charles, Brig.-Gen.	23
Chassery	25
Chastel Rouge	128, 130
Chauvel, Gen.	68, 150
Chaytor's Force	151
Cheshire, Sergt.	91
Chetwode, Gen.	68, 77, 98, 151
Chocolate Hill	138
Christie, Lieut.-Col. E. J.	2, 7, 13, 15, 159
Christie, Maj. O. F.	8, 13, 16
Cidemli	53
Cistern Bend	126, 127
Coggeshall	11
Craddock, Maj.	160
Crag, The	56
Crane, Sergt.	146
Croisette, La	20
Cross, Capt. J. J. B.	13, 16
Crump, Sergt.	90
Damascus	156
Davies, Lieut.	90
Davis, L./Cpl.	136
Dead Sea	129
De Beaurepaire, R.Q.M. Sergt.	161
Deir el Belah	64, 68
Deir Yesin	96
Derbasil	143
Devon trench	25
Doiran, Lake	57
Dollin, Sergt.	17
Dudular	43, 47, 57
Dumm, Wadi ed (Dumm, Talat ed, *see* T.)	117
Eames, Capt.	13
Earl, R.Q.M. Sergt.	161
Ecoivres	25, 28
Egerton, Capt.	143, 144
Ektief, Jebel	128
Elgood, Capt. V. A.	13, 96, 161
Enab	85, 94
Epsom Downs	9

	PAGE
Fara, Tel el	72
Feisul, Emir	133
Fejja	156
Ferdan, El	64
Ferguson, Lieut.-Gen. Sir Charles	22
Firmage, Pte.	89
Fry, Sergt.	119, 146
Ful, Tel el	100, 109, 116, 117

Gambell, Lieut.	144
Gardiner, Lieut.	128
Gatton Park	10
Gaza	59, 64, 66, 72, 77, 79, 83, 84, 122
Ghoraniyeh, El	133, 134, 135, 139, 141, 142, 143, 150
Ghuzzee, Wadi	70, 73, 77
Gray, Maj.	16, 48, 80, 82

Haifa	156
Haig, Sir Douglas	40
Harden, Lieut.	162
Hardwick, Pte.	136
Hardy, Lieut.	144
Hareira	79, 84
Hatfield	1
Hatfield Broad Oak	12, 16
Hatherley, Capt. E. J. W.	3, 13
Haud, El	139, 143
Haute Avesnes	25
Havre	19
Henderson, L./Cpl.	136
Hermaville	25
Hesi, Wadi	84
Highgate Ridge	149
Hill 535	47, 56, 57
Hobbs, Sergt.	138
Hobson, Capt. Neville	16, 29, 37, 52
Homs	157
Hood, 2nd Lieut.	127
Howeij	140
Hoxton, Pte.	136
Hubback, Maj. A. B.	3, 8
Hughes, Pte. T.	34
Huj	83
Hurcomb, Sergt.	98
Husk, Cpl.	91
Hythe	10

	PAGE
I Sector	56
Irgeig	81
Ismailia	60
Jaffa	84, 122, 157
Janes	47
Jeba	122, 123
Jemmameh, Wadi	84
Jericho	129, 142
Jerusalem	62, 84, 88, 93–113, 115, 122
Jones, 2nd Lieut. E.	138
Jones, 2nd Lieut. G. E.	134, 136
Jordan, River and Valley	125, 129, 131–147
Kalkilieh	156
Kantara	64, 157, 158
Karasuli	50, 56
Karm	73, 81
Kauwukah	79, 92
Kelly, Pte.	36
Kelt, Wadi	130
Kensington Gardens	6
Khan Khakun	129, 130
Khurbet Adaseh	114, 118
Khuweilfeh	79
Kubeibeh	85
Kustal	94, 95, 97, 98
Langley, Sergt.	54
Langlois, Sergt. W.	13, 92, 162
Latron	84
Lichfield Crater and Street	25, 37
Lifta	102
Lloyd, Sir Francis	8
Lothian Ravine	56
Mackay, Lieut.	136, 137
Makhadet Hajlah	134, 136
Maizieres	21
Manning, R.S.M. W.	3, 29, 160
Margrave, Cpl.	136
Marseilles	41
MacEwen, Capt.	4, 16
Mihalova	47, 57
Mitrailleuses, Crête des	55
Moascar	60, 62
Mont St. Eloi	25, 41
Morris, Lieut.	138
Morrison, Cpl.	32

		PAGE
Motley, The Rev. H.		144
Mount of Olives	112, 117, 124, 142,	148
Mukhmas		126
Mulebbis		157
Muntar, El		127
Musta, El		139, 140
Nablus		150, 154
Nahr el Falik		154
Naresh		46
Nasbeh, Tel el		118
Nazareth	150, 155,	156
Nebi Musa		129
Nebi Samwil	85, 87–91,	93
Neuville St. Vaast		25, 31
Newman, Capt.		8
Newton, Capt.		54
Norton, Lieut.-Col.		43, 160
"Nose, The"		55, 56
Olympus, Mount		45
Oreovica		55
Petit Houvin		20
Pickersgill, Pte.		90
Pitt, Sergt.		138
Plant, Cpl.		80
Pommerol, Capt.	13, 16,	54
Popham, L./Cpl.		136
Port Said		157
Porteous, Capt.		16
Powell, Pte.		136
R.A.M.C. Draft		18, 162
Radcliffe, Capt. C. N.	13, 37, 39, 48, 96, 122, 124, 134, 137, 143, 145,	146
Railway Clearing House		2, 3
Ram, Er	118,	121–123
Ram Allah		119, 148
Ras el Tawil		116, 118
Ratcliffe, Sergt.-Drummer		13
Regent's Park		4
Reigate		8
Reselli		53
Richmond Park		5, 8
Roberts, Pte.		39
Rogers, Pte.		18, 38
"Roosters"		110, 133
Roseveare, R. C.		16

	PAGE
Saffron Walden	13
St. Albans	11
Salamanli	47
Salonica	43, 57
Salt, Es	139, 140, 141, 143
Sarigol	47
Saris	94
Sarona	157
Scammell, Pte.	89, 146
Schonfield, Lieut.	36
Sebustiye	150
Sedgewick, Sergt.	98
Sejdelli	57
Selimli	53
Senussi	66
Shab Saleh	119, 121
Shafat	100, 114, 118
Sha'uth, El	70
Shea, Maj.-Gen. J. S. M.	69, 92, 94, 98, 107, 130, 149
Sheikh Nuran	70
Sheikh Selim	149
Sheppard, E. W.	6
Sheria	79–83
Shunet Nimrin	139, 143
Sidi Bishr	157
Signal Section	8, 13, 29, 71, 92, 135, 144, 161
Silver, L./Cpl.	136
Sims, Cpl.	138
Smol	55
Spancova Farm	47, 56
Speed, L./Cpl.	145
Stokes, Capt. J. G.	3, 4, 8
Studd, Brig.-Gen.	15, 35, 42
Suez Canal	64, 65
Suffa	125
Surar, Wadi	95, 97
Sutton Veney	14, 19
Sword, Lieut.-Col. D. C.	15, 29, 33, 42, 48, 52, 63, 80, 121, 159
Tabberner, Lieut. T. K.	13, 32, 35, 96, 98
Talat ed Dumm	125, 128–129, 130, 133, 134, 142
Targette, La	25
Templeton, Lieut.	122
Tennant, Capt. N. R. D.	16, 47, 50, 121, 125, 128
Torrens, Maj.	16
Totteridge	5
Tul Keram	150, 154–155

	PAGE
Vardar, River	49, 53, 55
Vardino	49, 51
Vimy Ridge	22, 31, 39
Vincent, Lieut.	80
Waggon Hill	56
Ward, Capt. F.	16, 36, 49, 92, 96, 98
Warr, Pte.	90
Watson, Gen. C. F.	74, 99, 153
Watson's Force	151
White City	5
White Hill	124–125
Whiting, Pte.	34
Williams, Lieut.	37, 38
Williamson, Maj. C. S.	13, 36, 55, 96, 153, 160
Windust, Sergt.	161
Woodroffe, Lieut.	134, 144
Woollaston, C. S. M.	17
Woodman, Cpl.	138
Yasur	157

LIST OF ILLUSTRATIONS.

	PAGE
Colours of the 19th London Regiment	FRONTISPIECE
Lt.-Col. Christie; Lt.-Col. Sword	4
Officers 2/19th London, Sutton Veney, 1916	12
Four Company Commanders	20
"D" Company H.Q. Dug-out, Neuville St. Vaast	31
A Crater Post, France	39
Beersheba—Turkish trenches, Hill 1070	76
Bridge Destroyed by Turks at Sheria	76
Two Methods of Conveying Wounded	84
Nebi Samwil—from the Turkish Positions	87
An Incident in the Capture of Jerusalem	93
Gen. Watson, Jaffa Gate, Jerusalem, 9/12/17	104
Jerusalem, Looking Towards the Mount of Olives	114
"B" Company, Talat ed Dumm	124
Talat ed Dumm—The Jericho Road Looking East	124
Pontoon Bridge—Makhadet-Hajlah, River Jordan	136
Refugees at Ghoraniyeh	136
Es Salt	142
Turks Making Road Between Jerusalem and Bethlehem	142
A Bivouac, Judean Hills	148
Turkish Deserters at Mezrah esh Sherkiyeh	148

LIST OF MAPS.

	PAGE
France, Divisional Area	18
France, 180th Brigade Sector, Vimy Ridge	28
Macedonia, XII Corps Front	42
Palestine, 1917–1918	64
Raids Across the Jordan	132